Simmonds on Bank Insurance

Insurance Advice for Community Bankers

Scott Simmonds, CPCU, ARM, CMC

Insurance from an Unbiased Point of View

(207) 284-0085 Fax (801) 991-4027

Scott@ScottSimmonds.com

www.ScottSimmonds.com

Bank Resource Center – www.BankInsuranceHelp.com

Published by Insurance Consultants of Maine, Inc.

Published in the United States
by Insurance Consultants of Maine, Inc.,
Saco, Maine

ISBN 0-9774015-2-9

Printed in the United States of America

Cover Design by GlairDesign

To my wife, Kathy, with love.

Thanks for supporting me in my work and life.

Contents

Introduction:

Every bank has insurance problems. Some know it. Some don't. Some will find out the hard way that they are missing an important coverage. Some will discover the problem from a review of their protection.

The exposures to loss faced by community banks are complex. It's an industry I have found interesting since my first coverage review for a building and loan association facing a regulatory takeover in 1984.

Banking is also an industry where my advice and skills are appreciated. I have found that many community banks use a local insurance agent who has little experience with the bond and liability insurance policies necessary to the banking industry. In many cases, the agents were glad I was called in; my services complement their work.

At the same time, I understand that not every bank needs my services. I wrote this book for the Presidents, VPs, CFOs, and CROs whose job it is to make insurance work for their institutions.

As a consultant, I approach the topic of insurance from a different perspective than most insurance experts. I started my consulting practice on the idea that insurance buyers should have someone on their side of the table. I never sell insurance. My advice isn't clouded by fees or commissions from insurance companies or insurance agents. I can recommend coverage from the full breadth of the marketplace. I'm unbiased. I work for insurance buyers.

I hope the information in this book is helpful to you. Feel free to let me know what you like and what you don't like about this guide. Call (207) 284-0085 or email me at Scott@ScottSimmonds.com. I'm interested in your thoughts and comments.

Scott Simmonds, CPCU, ARM, CMC
Saco, Maine
October, 2007

Chapter 1

General Insurance Issues

Review the Services Your Agent Offers

Insurance agents can be either employees of the insurance company for whom they sell (called direct writers), or independent business people who work for themselves. Independent agents usually represent more than one insurance company. While each will tell you that their approach is best, I find that both independent agents and direct writers have a place in the market.

Most community banks do business with independent agents. No two agencies have the same abilities or resources. No two agents have the same level of knowledge and expertise.

Make sure that your agent can meet your needs. Here are some questions to keep in mind when reviewing an agent's services:

- Who will manage your account on a daily basis? How long have the producer and service people been in the insurance business?
- Will the agent provide advice on all aspects of bank insurance?
- Does the agency have special expertise in banks and financial institutions?
- How are claims handled?
- Will one person in the agency oversee claim incident reports?
- Who will provide help preventing losses—the agent or the insurer?

It is common for banks to buy insurance from an agent who is a customer of the bank. Many banks use several agents to "spread the wealth." I've worked with banks where the property insurance is handled by one agent, auto by another, and directors' & officers' insurance by another. Consider this strategy carefully. You may be opening yourself up to misunderstandings of exposures and coverage. In such a setup, one agent may not know what coverage the other agents are providing. If you are going to work with multiple agents, consider building a list of coverages showing all policies. Share the list with all your agents so each knows what the others are doing.

My recommendation is usually that a business should have one insurance agent handle all the property and casualty insurance needs.

Insurance Is Not Gambling

Countless people, over the years, have told me that buying insurance is nothing more than gambling. Not true. Gambling creates risk, while insurance addresses and protects you from existing risk. When you gamble, you can finish in one of three places: a winner, a loser, or break even. You also can choose not to play.

Insurance addresses the risks you already face. You own a building. You must be sure it's still there tomorrow. The next day the building either is there or it's not. Insurance, unlike gambling, does not create risk.

Difference Between Insurance and Gambling

Gambling	Insurance
Creates risk	Addresses existing risk
Gain, loss, or stay even	No loss or loss

Insurance passes the risk of loss from you to the insurance company. That's why "self-insurance" is a misnomer. You either buy insurance or you don't. If you don't buy insurance you are funding the risk yourself, also known as "retention"; you retain the risk.

Be a Smart Insurance Buyer

Buying insurance requires taking time to understand what you need and what your policies cover. Follow the advice I received from an early mentor in my career: "The most important part of the insurance transaction is the relationship between the insurance agent and the client."

Do you feel comfortable with the information and advice your agent gives you? Does your agent know and understand bank insurance? Is your business appreciated? Do you feel well served when there's a problem? Follow your gut. If you don't have a good relationship with your insurer or agent, the results will be less than acceptable for you.

Your relationship with your agent is similar to that of your accountant and your lawyer. You must have faith that the agent has your best interests in mind. You must be confident that your agent is taking a proactive approach to your account. If you feel uncomfortable with the relationship, consider carefully if he or she is the best agent for you—even if they are a customer of the bank.

The most important part of the insurance transaction is the insurance buyer's relationship with their insurance agent.

Be an Exceptional Risk

Obtaining good insurance rates, in part, depends on you. Maintain your buildings. Insist on safe work habits. Train your employees to manage emergencies.

Put your best foot forward to your insurance company (current or potential) when inspectors show up. Housekeeping is important when insurers are evaluating your operation. Go on a pre-inspection walk-through looking at your operations, branches, and locations as an insurance company will. Make sure fire extinguishers are up to date and properly located. Electric panels and appliances should be installed correctly. Extension cords should be removed, or replaced by hardwired outlets. Pick up trash and clean up storage rooms.

Show insurers that you're a quality risk by having policies and procedures in place to control losses and manage claims.

Good Maintenance = Premium Credits

A bank client learned the hard way that housekeeping is important.

About three months before the renewal of the bank's package policy, the underwriter asked that the various locations be inspected by her loss control department. I told the CFO that the bank's maintenance team should do a thorough, pre-inspection walk-through to prevent any surprises. I gave him a rundown of the things the inspector would be looking for, including fire extinguishers, use of extension cords, fire safety issues, general housekeeping, electrical code violations, and a review of any cooking exposures or potential for loss, in employee break areas.

Several weeks later, I received a call from the bank's agent telling me that the underwriter had removed most of the premium credits for the upcoming package policy renewal. Apparently, the inspection had not gone well.

I urged the agent to get a copy of the deficiencies and ask the underwriter for an agreement that if all deficiencies were remedied within three weeks the credits would be returned to the policy.

The resulting premium credit to the policy was a savings of 15% to the bank.

Loss Prevention Is Always Your Best Tactic

Consider what you can do to prevent accidents and losses. How can you make your operation safer? It is always less expensive to prevent a loss than to have one. Inspect your properties regularly looking for problems. How would an insurance company inspector view your offices? What can be done to make the property safer and less prone to an accident or loss?

Consider ways to control the losses that do occur. Sprinkler systems minimize the damage caused by a fire. Expand your video surveillance system to show your parking lots. Having a clean desk policy in your administration center can limit the losses if the sprinkler or plumbing system fails. Exceptional data backup procedures limit downtime.

Look for practical ways to limit and prevent losses.

Consider Your Renewal Dates Carefully

The most popular renewal date for business insurance programs is January 1. July 1 is also common. The "quarter changes" of April and October are busy times for insurance companies, too.

Don't have your insurance renew anywhere near these dates. Underwriters and agents are scurrying around trying to handle three or four times their normal workload. Unless you are spending $1,000,000 a year on your insurance, you won't get the attention you deserve. If you currently have one of the above policy dates, consider changing it to a date like February 17 or June 12.

One exception ... Rarely do I recommend changing policy dates on workers' compensation policies. The experience modification calculation does not respond well to changing policy periods. See the section of this report on workers' compensation for more information.

Renewals – Use Competition in an Intelligent Way

At renewal, one agent quoting your policies with three insurers is not competition. Competition puts your agent and insurer in jeopardy of losing your business if they don't sharpen their pencils. It is only natural that an agent will work harder when there is the threat of losing you as a client.

Be cautious, however. Most insurers only provide quotes to one agent in a bid. It's called market blocking—insurers accept the first application submitted. No other agents can quote that insurer.

Having two agents attempting to access the same insurer creates conflict and infighting between the agents, which will hamper your bid efforts. Be sure the competing agents bring insurers into the bid process that your current agent can't access. Consider national specialty programs to compete with your local agent. This adds a different flavor to the bid process. Direct writers such as Liberty Mutual can help, too.

An integral part of the bid process is your control over which agent uses which insurance company. More info on this topic can be found in the section of this book on the bid process.

A Downside to Bidding

I've outlined above the conflict that can occur when two agents access the same insurer. Assigning insurers to specific agents also can lead to imperfect combinations of coverage.

The best insurance program does not always come from one insurance company. Perhaps Company A has the best auto program while Company B has the best package policy. If you assign Company A to Agent A and company B to Agent B, you will not be able to use one agent for the all-around best insurance program. You could cherry-pick. However, using two agents comes with its own set of troubles.

For more information on the bid process, see chapters 19, 20, and 21.

Consider Competition without Bidding

The traditional bid process may not be the best approach to getting the best insurance program. A broker selection process allowing presentations from several agents can work well. Each broker outlines their approach and services. Sometimes a conceptual proposal that includes a broker's suggestions on coverage and service improvements is the best approach.

Build a list of agents who you think can provide the service and expertise you require. Get names from colleagues and other bankers. Prepare a summary of your current insurance, including insurers and premiums, along with a detailed description of your business. Prepare a questionnaire that agents can complete. Ask about services provided, résumés of the people who will handle the account, and insurers who will work with you.

See the appendix for forms to help with the broker selection process.

Review Coverage for Value

Review all your insurance coverage to determine the true value in light of current premium levels. Many banks added earthquake, flood, and machinery breakdown coverage in years past. Is the coverage worth the current premium? Are your premium dollars better spent in other areas? Is the cost of the coverage worth the value of the protection? Consider catastrophic losses as you review your insurance for value.

Start the Policy Renewal Process Early

You'll need at least 90 days to "work" the renewal of your insurance program. If you're getting quotes from other agents, it will take time to develop bid specs and gather the information and data that underwriters will need.

Even if you're not bidding, talk with your insurance agent early. He or she should know what your current insurer is planning. Ask about premiums and coverage. Many carriers add exclusions and restrictions to renewal policies. Get at least a ballpark renewal quote as early as possible. Push your agent and insurer. You're the customer!

Review Your Insurer's Financial Ratings

Each year, insurance companies go out of business. In the past 20 years, more than 600 insurers became insolvent, severely impacting their clients. Claims went unpaid. Policies had to be replaced quickly, resulting in lower coverage and higher premiums—not a fun time.

Several organizations analyze insurance companies for soundness. The best known is the AM Best Company (www.ambest.com). Standard & Poor's also rates insurers. I rely on TheStreet.com Ratings (also called Weiss Ratings) (www.TheStreet.com) as a tough, unbiased source of information. They never accept fees from insurers. They utilize industry and regulators' filings in their analyses. They're tough graders; a B- is still considered good in their system.

A recent review of AM Best Ratings revealed that almost 90 percent of insurance companies receive a rating of "Very Good" or better. Only 29 percent of insurers received a Weiss Rating of "Good" or better. I believe that Weiss has a higher standard. When working with my clients' money, I want objective, tough, and accurate ratings.

An insolvent insurer means your coverage is compromised. Use rating organizations such as AM Best and Weiss Ratings to help you make informed decisions.

Remember the Pollution Exclusion

Over the past 20 years, the insurance industry has been hammered by the courts on pollution claims. The result is that most standard insurance policies have pollution exclusions so broad that the industry calls them "absolute pollution exclusions."

Liability arising out of pollution is excluded by most general liability insurance policies. If the oil tank for your heating system leaks and pollutes your neighbor's well, there is no coverage. Directors' and officers' policies also have pollution exclusions.

Your property insurance probably has an exclusion for damage to your property caused by pollution—your pollution or pollution caused by others.

The only exception to the above is for the cleanup of pollution on your premises caused by a peril included in your property insurance. Coverage is usually limited to $25,000.

Pollution Cleanup Expense Example

In most insurance policies, the only pollution coverage is for the cleanup of a spill caused by an insured event at your premises.

Example event: Ice from your roof falls and severs the fuel line of an outside oil tank that runs to your heating system. One hundred and fifty gallons of heating oil spill onto the ground.

The state environmental protection agency requires that the contaminated soil is removed and trucked to a special landfill. Monitoring is mandated and the hole must be left open for three months to assure complete removal of contaminants. Total cost is $20,000.

Hints for Reading Your Insurance Policies

The mere thought of reading an insurance policy can make a banker's head hurt. Here are some hints to make it less painful.

Start with an understanding of the purpose of the insurance policy. An auto policy is designed to cover vehicle accidents. General liability insurance is purchased to protect the insured from liability arising out of bodily injury, property damage, personal injury, and advertising injury. Directors' and officers' insurance indemnifies the key people for errors in judgment and bad decisions.

Read the declarations page, usually the first few pages of the policy. It will have information specific to the policy being reviewed, such as: policy effective and cancellation dates; name of insured; the subject of the insurance policy (list of vehicles, buildings, description of property, etc.); premiums charged; policy form numbers and edition dates.

Words in bold print or within quotation marks are defined by the policy. For example, in a general liability policy the word "bodily injury" is defined in a separate section of the policy. Find the definitions section and browse the terms.

Read the insuring agreement. This is usually the first part of the actual policy wording. It will tell you what is covered by the policy.

For property insurance, learn what causes of loss are insured. For a directors' and officers' insurance policy, look at the definition of "wrongful act."

Review the exclusions to learn what is not covered by the policy. Most policies start with broad insuring agreements, then whittle away at the coverage with the use of exclusions. Broad exclusions are not necessarily bad. For example, a general liability policy will exclude auto accidents. No problem. That's why you buy an auto insurance policy.

While reviewing exclusions, look for exceptions to the exclusion. Look for wording like, "This exclusion does not apply to ...." For example, the general liability policy excludes watercraft. There is an exception to the exclusion in most policies for watercraft less than 26 feet in length that you do not own.

Review the endorsements (usually found at the end of the policy) for amendments to the standard policy language. It is not unusual to have more than ten endorsements to the policy. The title of the endorsement usually gives you a good idea of what the form is trying to accomplish. If an endorsement deletes a section of the policy, mark that section in the policy document for future reference.

Review policy conditions to learn the general "rules of the road" for the policy. Issues like cancellation, arbitration, and claims reporting are usually covered in this section.

I read insurance policies with a pencil in hand. I mark sections and summarize the contents of a particular clause in two or three words.

Chapter 2

Property Insurance

Property insurance includes coverage on your buildings, the contents of your buildings, and the loss of income that comes from a fire or other insured cause of loss. There also can be coverage for the increased cost of getting back into business quickly.

How Is Property Valued?

The value of your buildings, contents, and other business property can be determined in many ways:

- Real estate value (the price you could sell at)
- Tax assessment value
- Replacement cost
- Book value (purchase price minus accounting depreciation)

- Actual cash value (replacement cost minus usage depreciation)

Two forms of valuation are used in property insurance. The traditional (meaning old-fashioned) valuation is "actual cash value." The term is defined by most policies as replacement cost minus depreciation. In some states, you must also consider market value in the determination of the actual cash value of property.

Actual Cash Value – Building Example

Suppose that a 30-year-old building would cost $1,500,000 to replace. The structure is well maintained and in no way obsolete. The roof was replaced last year. Plumbing and electrical have been updated recently. A fire destroys the building.

The insurance company adjuster determines that 20% depreciation is called for. She issues a check to the insured for $1,500,000, less 20%, minus the deductible.

Actual Cash Value – Personal Property Example

Suppose that a pipe in the ceiling of a bank branch office bursts, damaging a conference table, chairs, audiovisual equipment, and several computers. The cost to replace the items is $35,000.

The insurance company adjuster determines that the equipment was obsolete and the furniture was in poor repair. Based on photographs and interviews it is determined that 60% depreciation is in order. You are offered $14,000 (40% of $35,000), less your deductible.

Replacement cost valuation within property insurance looks at the replacement cost of a building. How much will it cost to rebuild the building if it burned to the ground using the current cost of materials and labor?

Ninety percent of the time, you want your insurance to be written on a replacement cost basis. The policy agrees to pay the full cost of reconstruction without deduction for depreciation.

In rare instances, you will insure a building for its actual cash value. My recommendation is to carry actual cash value coverage only when you would not replace a building after a fire, a relatively rare plan.

Personal property also can be valued at replacement cost or on its actual cash value. Again, in most cases, replacement cost is the most desirable valuation.

Buy the Right Amount of Coverage

Most property policies have severe penalties for underinsurance. The amount of coverage you buy depends on the valuation of the property. Most banks need replacement cost coverage—insurance designed to pay for the replacement of your property with new materials and the current cost of labor.

Your agent can help you with estimating the replacement cost of your buildings.

Determining the value of contents is tougher. I recommend you go through your locations room by room and count thousands of dollars in value (desk and chair, $1,000; three file cabinets, $1,000; computer and printer, $2,000).

Beware of Coinsurance

Coinsurance is a penalty provision found in most property insurance policies for underinsurance. It never helps you. It can only hurt at the time of a loss.

Example – Underinsured Building with Coinsurance

Property value: $1,000,000

80% coinsurance clause (requires the purchase of $800,000 of insurance)

Amount of insurance: $750,000

Amount of fire loss: $75,000

Loss calculation: What you bought, divided by what you should have bought, times the amount of the loss.

Claim payment = $750,000 divided by $800,000 = .9375

.9375 multiplied by $75,000 = $70,313

$75,000 - $70,313 = $4,687 Coinsurance penalty

Example – Correctly Insured Building with Coinsurance

Property value: $1,000,000

80% coinsurance clause (requires the purchase of $800,000 of insurance)

Amount of insurance: $850,000

Amount of fire loss: $75,000

Since the amount of insurance is more than the $800,000 required by coinsurance, the loss payment is the full $75,000 (less any deductible).

Most insurers will eliminate the coinsurance clause at your request. Many carriers will add a clause to the policy agreeing that the amount of insurance meets the coinsurance clause—called the agreed amount endorsement. Work with your agent to eliminate any coinsurance clauses from your policies.

Blanket Insurance

Talk with your agent about blanket coverage—one amount of insurance for all your property. Even if your bank is contained in only one building, combining the building and contents insurance into one amount of coverage can help you at the time of a claim.

Example – Specific Insurance

Main building coverage: $1,700,000

Contents of main building: $750,000

Elm Street branch building coverage: $750,000

Contents of Elm Street branch: $400,000

If the Elm Street location burned, the policy would pay up to $750,000 for the repair of the building and $400,000 for the replacement of the contents.

Example – Blanket Insurance

Main building coverage: $1,700,000

Contents of main building: $750,000

Elm Street branch building coverage: $750,000

Contents of Elm Street branch: $400,000

Blanket amount of insurance: $3,600,000 (1,700,000+750,000+750,000+400,000)

If the Elm Street location burned, the policy would pay up to $3,600,000 for the repair of the building and for the replacement of the contents.

Special Perils

Perils are causes of loss—fire, lightning, wind, hail. Policies that include coverage for "special perils" provide the broadest coverage—protection for any cause of loss not excluded by the policy. Common exclusions are earthquake, flood, nuclear events, damage by insects or animals, and mold. If the cause of loss is not excluded by the policy, there is coverage for the damage.

So-called "named peril" policies provide a laundry list of events for which coverage applies: fire, lightning, hail, vehicles, aircraft, windstorm, explosion, vandalism, for example. If the damage was caused by a peril not listed, there is no coverage.

Put another way, special perils policies cover any cause of loss except what is excluded. Named peril policies cover only causes of loss listed.

"Special perils" is the preferable way to write a property insurance policy.

Machinery Coverage – The Peril of Mechanical Breakdown

Many property insurance policies are now including a new peril that was previously excluded: mechanical breakdown.

Some banks have a "boiler and machinery" policy that provides equivalent coverage. I include a discussion here, as you may find the protection within your property policy.

Consider the events that will cause you to have to replace a phone system, air-conditioning plant, heating system, or other machines and equipment.

Clearly, fire, theft, vandalism, or a windstorm that destroys your building can damage the equipment. All these perils are covered by your property insurance.

How about a voltage surge that blows out the motor of your air-conditioning system? How about loss of water in a heating system that causes a crack in the boiler? How about the failure of the lubrication system in an elevator unit that causes overheating and damage to the travel unit?

All of the above are excluded by standard property insurance.

Machinery coverage (a separate policy or an added peril to the property policy) can add protection for the losses described.

Machinery Coverage Comment

In general, banks have little need for machinery coverage. The largest loss I have seen in a bank for machinery or mechanical breakdown is $3,500 for the replacement of certain components in an alarm system when a voltage surge hit the system. Certainly not a catastrophic loss. Inconvenient? Yes. The bank didn't lose any business, though, and the alarm was up and running that afternoon.

I'm not saying no bank should ever buy machinery coverage.

If your building is heated with a high-pressure boiler, buy the coverage 100% of the time. Otherwise, look at the value of the coverage and your other insurance needs. Is the premium for machinery coverage better spent on additional umbrella liability coverage or additional limits on your bond or your D&O protection?

<u>What's a Building?</u>

On its face, the word "building" seems straightforward. Not in the world of insurance.

Most property insurance policies define "building" as the structure described in the policy, including:

- Completed additions;
- Fixtures including outdoor fixtures;
- Permanently installed machinery and equipment;
- Personal property owned by you that is used to maintain or service the building, including fire extinguishing equipment, outdoor furniture, floor coverings, and appliances used for refrigerating, ventilating, cooking, dishwashing, or laundering.

While the policy does not define "fixtures," it's generally held to be items such as light poles and flagpoles, parking stops, mailboxes, and in-ground sprinkler systems. Signs attached to your building are also considered fixtures. A drive-through awning is a part of the building. The pneumatic tubes at drive-up windows are covered as part of the building. Most insurers would consider an ATM unit to be a fixture—even as a separate kiosk.

ATMs in a separate building should be separately insured and described in most policies.

Under most insurance policies, freestanding signs would be covered only to $250 or other small amount. Extra coverage can be purchased.

Additions under construction are covered—if you have not purchased other insurance such as builder's risk.

Materials used in construction of the addition are covered when stored within 100 feet of the premises.

Consider Flood Insurance

Earlier, I said that flood is excluded from most property insurance policies. Don't think of it as water damage. Floodwater is not nice clean water. Floods take out septic systems and sewage treatment plants. Dead things will be floating in the basement of your building. Shovels, not mops, are used to clean up the mess. It's dirty, smelly, and disgusting. You'll want help cleaning it up, and insurance offers that help.

Many insurers will offer flood coverage as part of the package policy. You'll probably have a separate limit. Perhaps the policy will include a limit of $1,000,000 for any location. Is that enough?

Some policies provide coverage for flood only to buildings not located in flood zones. Check your policy.

Consider Earthquake Insurance

Earthquake is excluded under most property insurance policies. Consider adding coverage for this peril.

If you live in quake-prone areas, your agent has undoubtedly discussed the coverage with you. Most agents on the East Coast don't even talk about earthquake with their clients. That can be a mistake.

Intense quakes can hit anywhere. An earthquake hit Boston in 1755 that damaged 1,200 buildings. More than 100 chimneys were leveled. People on ships in the harbor said they felt like they had run aground, the intensity was so great. Think what would happen if that same intensity earthquake hit Boston now.

Talk with your agent. You may be surprised how inexpensive the coverage is.

Business Interruption and Extra Expense

I am regularly asked to explain business income insurance. First, let's get past semantics. The following terms mean the same thing: business interruption coverage, loss of business income, time element, use and occupancy. They all describe protection from the loss of income that occurs when a business is shut down due to a fire or other insured loss.

Silly Story to Explain Loss of Business Income Insurance

For many years I've used the same story to help business owners understand what exactly business income coverage does. It's a silly story but it makes my point.

Pretend you own a goose (a building). Your goose lays golden eggs (cash flow). If your goose is run over by a truck, it's going to take you nine months to get a new goose (get back into operation). You have insurance that will pay for the cost of the new goose (property insurance), but what about the value of the eggs you won't get in the nine months you're without a goose? Business income coverage pays the value of the eggs while you're waiting for your new goose.

Part two of business interruption coverage is extra expense—coverage that pays the increased cost of getting your goose in five months instead of waiting nine. It is the most pressing need for business interruption coverage for banks. If a branch is down due to fire or windstorm, the priority is to reopen quickly through a temporary location or bank trailer. Extra expense coverage will pay for the rental.

Insurers will generally provide a blanket limit of extra expense coverage over all locations. Work with your advisor to determine the correct business income protection for you.

Another point: Eliminate coinsurance penalties from business income coverage, if possible.

Deductibles

I find that most banks have relatively low deductibles. Think of it this way: Your home insurance probably has a $500 or $1,000 deductible and a few hundred thousand in insurance. Your bank has millions of dollars of insurance. Does a $1,000 deductible really make sense?

Things happen in our daily lives. Don't use your insurance to pay for the bumps in the road. Look to insurance to help you through catastrophes.

Did vandals damage a sign outside the main office? Why look to insurance to pay for it? Did a windstorm damage a few shingles on the roof of a branch office? Fix them and move on. Insurance should be for when your roof is destroyed or for a loss that would have a devastating effect on your bank's financial health.

Use high deductibles on your property insurance to reduce your premiums. Consider $5,000, $10,000 or higher. Small losses are a cost of business. Budget for them.

Note: Never pay liability claims yourself. Report damage to other people's property or injuries to people as soon as possible. Even if it seems that the injury is minor, report the claim to your insurer quickly.

Storage Locations

Review other locations where you may have property, such as warehouses and mini-warehouses. Consider equipment that may belong to the bank that is at employees' homes. Telecommuters and executives with bank computers at home may need to be listed on your property insurance policies.

Computer Coverage

Some property insurers segregate computers into a separate limit of coverage. Are your computers properly covered? Is the limit of insurance adequate? Is a computer virus a covered cause of loss? Does the policy include coverage for laptops and other computer equipment that is away from a bank premises? Is there coverage for PDAs and hand-held computers?

Builder's Risk Insurance

The construction of a new building usually requires specific insurance to address the hazards encountered in construction. Talk with your insurance advisor and contractor about your need for builder's risk insurance.

See the separate section of this book for details of builder's risk insurance.

Property Insurance Exclusions

Most bank property insurance is written on a "special perils" basis (see the earlier discussion on the workings of perils). In short, the policy says every cause of loss is included except what is excluded. Here's the normal list of excluded perils:

- ordinance or law
- earth movement
- governmental action
- nuclear hazards
- utility service
- war and military action
- water
- artificially-generated electrical currents
- delay, loss of use, and loss of market
- wear and tear, mechanical breakdown
- changes in temperature or humidity

- explosion of steam boiler or pressure vessel
- continuous or repeated leakage of water
- loss by freezing (unless you take precautions)
- dishonest or criminal acts by you or employees (except for acts of destruction)
- voluntary parting
- rain, snow, ice, or sleet to personal property in the open
- pollution
- acts or decisions
- faulty, inadequate, or defective planning, design, repair, materials or maintenance

The policy also describes property that is not covered. The excluded items relevant to banks are:

- accounts, bills, currency, money, notes
- cost of excavations
- foundations, land, retaining walls
- property covered by another policy
- underground pipes
- fences, radio antennas, satellite dishes

Vacant Property Issues

A vacant building has coverage restrictions. After a building has been vacant for 60 consecutive days, coverage for the following perils is excluded:

- vandalism
- sprinkler leakage / water damage
- glass breakage
- theft or attempted theft

Perhaps the Most Common Bank Property Loss?

Banks don't have a great many property losses. In my career, though, I have seen four banks with the same incident. It's a silly event and the cause of much embarrassment for all concerned—a truck getting stuck in the drive-through teller roof overhang.

Loss prevention is simple for this type of accident. Put up a sign or a hanging tube for the unwary to hit before they hit your building.

Valuable Papers Insurance

Valuable papers insurance pays for the cost of recreating documents destroyed by an insured peril. It pays for the cost of research and copying the documents you need to run your business after a fire or other insured cause of loss.

Example: Fire destroys part of your office space that contains important records. The information is vital to your operation and to your regulators. The data must be recreated. Valuable papers insurance will pay the restoration costs.

However, buying valuable papers insurance is a lousy way to protect your bank's records. Physically protect documents or records that are important to your operation. Put your vital documents in fireproof filing cabinets or a vault. Better yet, scan paper records and store them digitally—with proper backup, of course!

Debris Removal

After a fire or other insured damage to your building, there likely will be debris that needs to be removed. Coverage is usually limited to 25 percent of the loss. The amounts paid for debris removal do not increase the total limit of coverage for the whole claim. It is, therefore, possible that you can run out of coverage.

To help, insurers provide an additional amount of coverage (usually $10,000) to pay for the cleanup. Some insurance companies increase the additional amount to $25,000 or $50,000.

Review your buildings. Will special disposal of rubble and debris increase the cost of reconstruction? Asbestos or other hazardous substances (found in older buildings) may point to the need for additional insurance.

Fine Arts

If your bank owns artwork, antiques, or other items of unusual value, consider having the items appraised and insured under a fine arts policy.

Fine arts insurance provides additional perils (breakage, for example) and alternative valuation methods (cost of restoration) to what is offered by standard insurance policies.

Highly valued windows, murals, and other ornamentation can be specifically insured also.

Don't forget to insure artwork loaned to museums and galleries. Check the loan agreement; you may find that the receiving institution is responsible for coverage.

Signs

Signs attached to your buildings are covered by most standard building insurance. Freestanding signs need to be insured specifically or with a special policy endorsement.

Mail Insurance

Mail insurance protects property in the custody of a government postal service. Review the policy for specific descriptions of property covered and who may be transporting the property. Some policies will extend coverage to include organizations like Federal Express and UPS.

Chapter 3

Builder's Risk Insurance

Builder's risk insurance policies cover buildings during construction, renovation or repair. Insurance coverage is provided on the structure and materials used in construction. In most cases, materials are covered while in transit, at temporary storage locations, and while stored at the job site. Here are some of the issues to consider:

Who Is Buying the Coverage?

In many instances, your contractor will obtain the builder's risk coverage for you. Make sure you are listed as an insured on the policy and that the coverage is broad enough to cover your exposures—specifically, soft costs and loss of business income.

You May Already Have Coverage

Your property insurance policy may include coverage for newly acquired and newly constructed buildings. The amount of insurance may be relatively small. However, it may be broad enough to eliminate the need for an additional insurance policy. Review your policy for the perils included in the coverage.

Amount of Coverage

Most policies require that you include 100 percent of the expected construction cost as the amount of insurance. Coinsurance penalties may apply if you fail to meet this requirement. Work with your insurance advisor to determine what costs to include in selecting the amount of builder's risk coverage.

Deductibles

Higher deductibles can reduce your insurance costs. Consider $5,000, $10,000 or more.

Perils Covered

What causes of loss are included in the policy? Special perils insurance forms include damage by any cause except what's excluded—earthquake, flood, intentional damage by you, mold, terrorism, and damage by insects or vermin, for example. Named peril policies list the events that are covered—fire, lightning, wind, explosion ....

Consider Flood and Earthquake Coverage

Damage caused by flood and earthquake is usually excluded from basic policies. Get quotes and consider the coverage.

Exclusions

In addition to the flood and earthquake exclusions mentioned, most policies will not cover damage caused by defect in construction, defect in design, mold, pollution, settling, cracking, shrinking, bulging, or expansion.

Theft of Building Materials

Some builder's risk insurance policies exclude theft of building materials stored on site. Some require gated storage areas. Read your policy.

Subcontractors' Work

Is the work of subcontractors (while in process) included in the coverage?

Collapse During Construction

Some policies exclude damage caused in the collapse of the building. Review your insurance policy.

Business Income

Coverage can be included for loss of income in the event that a fire or other insured event prevents you from doing business. Imagine a new hotel under construction that is destroyed two months before completion. The losses in revenue while the building is rebuilt could be substantial. Work with your insurance advisor on the correct amount of loss of business income coverage you should have.

Liability Insurance

Builder's risk insurance does not include coverage for bodily injury or damage to property of others. Look to your general liability insurance for protection.

Get Quotes

Your insurance agent or broker can get you quotes. For new construction, your agent should get proposals from several insurers. There are specialty programs for builder's risk insurance which may offer a better price and coverage.

Work with your contractor and architect to determine who should purchase the builder's risk coverage.

<u>Occupancy</u>

Most builders' risk insurance coverage terminates at occupancy. Coverage ends automatically. Be sure you let your agent know ahead of time that you are moving in. Coverage may terminate if the building is ready for occupancy. Talk with your advisor.

<u>Soft Costs</u>

After a building under construction is destroyed, there may be architects' fees, attorneys' bills, planning board reviews, and the like before reconstruction can begin. Many policies require soft costs to be a separate limit of coverage.

Chapter 4

General Liability Insurance

The purpose of general liability insurance is to provide protection for bodily injury and property damage that come out of the operation of your bank. The policy will provide coverage for slip and fall claims and other accidents. Most policies also include coverage for personal injury—libel, slander, defamation, wrongful arrest.

- A customer falls on your walkway or parking lot.
- An employee accidentally injures a customer.
- A piece of candy you give away makes a customer sick.
- An employee wrongly accuses a customer of theft.

Coverage Overview and Limits

There are several limits of coverage in most general liability policies.

Occurrence Limit

Coverage amount that is available for each occurrence or accident. One million dollars is the usual minimum limit.

General Aggregate Limit

Total coverage available for the combination of all occurrences in a policy period. At a minimum you will want two times your occurrence limit here. Three times is better.

Products Aggregate Limit

Total coverage available for the combination of all product liability occurrences in a policy period. Should be two or three times the occurrence limit.

Personal Injury

Coverage available for a personal injury occurrence—libel, slander, defamation, wrongful eviction, false arrest. The coverage amount is usually the same as the occurrence limit.

Fire Damage Liability

Coverage for damage to a building you occupy or rent from others – also called fire legal liability. The general liability policy excludes damage to property in your care, custody, or control. Fire Damage Liability brings back protection for damage to property you occupy but don't own. Most policies provide $50,000 but you may need more.

Medical Payments

Coverage for medical bills incurred because of an accident at your premises. Pays regardless of fault or liability. I call this "goodwill coverage." If you were negligent, you turn to the coverage per occurrence, above. "Med pay" is most often used for slip and fall accidents. The most common coverage limit is $5,000, although more is available.

Exclusions

Here are the common issues not covered by general liability insurance:

- Pollution (for coverage, buy pollution insurance)
- Employment practices – discrimination, wrongful discharge (buy employment practices insurance)
- Asbestos, mold, and fungi
- Employee benefit plan errors (buy fiduciary responsibilities liability insurance)
- Professional liability (buy professional liability insurance)
- Injuries to employees (covered by workers' compensation)
- Automobiles (covered by auto insurance)
- Aircraft – both owned and non-owned
- Owned watercraft and non-owned watercraft over 26 feet

- Liquor liability for those in the business of making, selling or serving alcohol

<u>General Issues</u>

Review the coverage to be sure protection is extended to holding companies, subsidiaries, and any charitable foundations managed by your bank.

Contractors working for the bank should provide certificates of liability, workers' compensation, and auto liability insurance. Data processing operations and contractors working on your computer systems should provide evidence of professional liability insurance.

Review your bank's use of watercraft. I know this sounds strange. Many banks, however, host chamber of commerce functions or customer/employee events on large party boats. The standard general liability coverage limitation for a non-owned boat is 26 feet. You may also have loan officers or executives with large boats. Entertaining bank customers or employees may be a normal part of business. If the boat is over 26 feet, the bank may be exposed to a lawsuit should an accident occur.

<u>Pollution Exclusions</u>

Most general liability policies exclude coverage for any form of pollution liability.

- The bank's heating oil tank leaks into the neighbor's basement—no coverage.

- A gas station the bank owns through a foreclosure has a leaky storage tank—no coverage.

Special pollution liability policies are available. Few banks purchase such coverage. Look at your own situation. Identify possible sources of pollution and take action to prevent incidents (regular fuel tank inspections). Review the hazards that exist on foreclosed properties.

Liability Coverage for Special Events

The general liability insurance policy provides broad protection for bodily injury and damage to the property of others that arise out of your bank's normal operation. Coverage includes your day-to-day activities and special events such as customer appreciation events, anniversary celebrations, and community event sponsorships. There is generally no need to buy special coverage to protect the bank for these types of parties.

Invasion of Privacy

Violations of privacy become a greater issue almost every day. Look to your general liability insurance for coverage under the personal and advertising injury section.

Most policies will specifically include coverage for "oral or written publication, in any manner, of material that violates a person's right of privacy." There is a standard exclusion for "personal and advertising injury caused by or at the direction of the insured with the knowledge that the act would violate the rights of another and would inflict personal and advertising injury."

Some insurers are adding exclusions for damages caused by an invasion of privacy. Review your policy.

Chapter 5

Automobile Insurance

The business auto policy is straightforward. It covers the bank's exposure to liability claims from autos owned or leased by the bank. It should also cover the bank's liability for damages caused by employees who drive personal vehicles on bank business. Repossessed vehicles and customers' leased and rented vehicles are also an issue.

Physical damage insurance protects the bank for damage to the vehicles—so-called comprehensive and collision insurance.

Automobile Liability

This part of your auto insurance provides protection for the injuries you cause (bodily injury) and the damage you do to other people's property (property damage). One million dollars of auto liability coverage should be the minimum limit for banks.

The coverage symbol should be "any auto" or at least must include hired and non-owned autos. See section below for info on the coverage symbols used in most policies.

Uninsured Motorists/Underinsured Motorists

Uninsured/Underinsured motorists insurance pays for the injuries to you and others in your car, caused by a driver with either no insurance or too little insurance. Your insurer pays you, then "goes after" the other person.

Coverage availability varies by state. In most cases, it is best to have the limit of uninsured motorist coverage the same as your liability coverage. Recall that injured employees (while working) are probably covered by workers' compensation.

Personal Injury Coverage

Also known as "no-fault" or PIP insurance. It pays for your medical bills caused by an auto accident. Under no-fault, you don't need to sue the other party. This coverage section is not a part of auto insurance in all states.

Medical Payments

Pays the medical bills for people in your vehicle when there is an accident. In most states this coverage is limited to some relatively small amount—$1,000 or $5,000. It can pay the deductibles and co-payments of your health insurance.

Comprehensive

Also called "Other than Collision." This part of your auto insurance pays for the damage to your car caused by something other than an accident—fire, hail, windstorm, theft, or vandalism, for example. The coverage section also pays for the damage to your car caused by hitting an animal (not considered an accident but an act of God). There is usually a deductible stated—the amount you pay in the event of an accident.

Use a large deductible to control premiums. Consider not buying comprehensive coverage if your vehicle is more than five model years old.

Collision

Pays for the damage to your car or truck that has been in an accident. The policy will include an amount you pay before the insurance company steps in—a deductible. Use a large deductible to control premiums.

Consider not buying collision coverage if your vehicle is more than five model years old.

Towing & Labor Insurance

Pays for the cost of towing and labor expenses when your vehicle is disabled. Usually limited to some small amount—$35, for example. Usually not worth the premium. Don't turn in small property claims!

Rental Vehicle Coverage

Pays for the rental of a car after an accident. What would you do if a particular vehicle were taken out of commission? This is another area of low severity. It may be a part of an extension endorsement provided by your insurer.

Auto Extension Endorsements

Many insurers have a policy endorsement that extends protection to other areas. Coverage can include life insurance, additional medical payments, payments for remaining lease installments, and extending the coverage for a car you rent. Talk with your agent about your policy.

Non-Owned Auto Coverage

It isn't just the cars you own that expose your bank to liability. Every time an employee goes to a meeting or visits with a customer, the bank is exposed. If a loan officer causes an accident while driving his own vehicle on bank business, the bank could be sued. Check with your agent to be sure you have non-owned auto coverage.

Drive Other Car Coverage

Protects employees who are provided company cars and don't have their own personal auto policy. Talk with your agent. You may get this coverage automatically if you buy the coverage broadening endorsement offered by many insurance companies.

Renting Cars

When renting cars (short-term rentals from Hertz and Avis, for example), buy the coverage offered by the rental car company or use a credit card that provides the same insurance. Call your credit card customer service department for the details of your credit card company's service.

Damage to Employee Vehicles

What are employees' expectations for damage caused in accidents while driving their personal vehicles? Will you pay for damage to their vehicle or should the employee rely upon their own insurance? Will you pay their deductible? Make your plan clear in your employee handbook to avoid misunderstandings. Send an annual reminder to all employees stating your bank's policy on employee vehicle usage.

Use Same Insurer for Auto and General Liability

Consider having the same insurer for auto and general liability to eliminate any coverage gaps or overlaps.

Repossessed Vehicles

How are repossessed cars covered by your auto policy? "Any auto" liability coverage will protect the bank. How about damage to the vehicles—comprehensive and collision insurance? A repossessed vehicle is considered an owned vehicle by most insurers. You may be able to add coverage to your bank's auto policy. Talk with your agent.

Parking Garages

Is the exposure for your parking garage covered? Parking vehicles may expose the bank to claims that you are responsible for any damage that occurs. This is certainly true if you charge a fee for parking. What are employees' expectations of payment for damage to their vehicles while parked in the bank's parking lot? Talk with your agent about garagekeepers insurance.

Coverage Symbols

Commercial auto policies specify the extent of coverage provided by using numeric symbols to indicate the breadth of the protection.

The declarations page of your auto policy outlines coverage areas (liability, uninsured motorist, medical payments, etc.) with coverage symbols that apply to the type of insurance. The applicable symbols are numbers 1 through 9.

Symbol 1 is the broadest—any auto. Symbol 9 provides coverage for non-owned vehicles only. Using symbol 7 reduces the coverage to claims from vehicles listed on the policy only. Insurers sometimes use a combination of symbols, 8 and 9, for example, to provide coverage for hired and non-owned autos.

Symbol 1 in the liability section would provide coverage for any auto liability claim brought against an insured. Symbol 7 in the liability section would limit liability coverage to claims that come from a vehicle listed on the policy—significantly restricting the coverage.

Chapter 6

Workers' Compensation

For many banks, workers' compensation insurance is a huge expense and hassle. The policy is a straightforward way that employees can be compensated for workplace injuries. It is, truly, a no-fault insurance policy.

Your bank pays a premium based on your payroll and past loss experience. The insurance company handles any claims that occur. The detail of the premium calculation is where there are opportunities for mistakes and savings.

Importance of Correct Classification

Review your policy classifications for accuracy. Work with your agent to be sure that the classes and rates you have are correct for your operation. Ask your agent for a copy of the Scopes® description of your classifications. Most bank employees will be classified as "clerical." Maintenance and courier drivers will be separately rated. There also may be a separate sales code for commercial lenders, and other marketing people who are on the road.

Understand the Definition of Payroll

Make sure your insurer isn't charging you for payroll that should not be included. For example, the extra wages you pay for overtime work should be removed. Your executive officers' payrolls may be eligible for capping at a maximum wage. Talk with your insurance advisor.

Get Copies of Your Audit Worksheets

Ask your insurer to provide you with a copy of the Audit Worksheet prepared for your most recently expired policy. This document provides the details of how the insurance company determined your final premium. It lists employees, classifications, and payrolls. Look for errors such as the inclusion of overtime and incorrect classification of employees.

Consider Deductibles

Consider using a substantial deductible to control your premiums. Work with your agent to determine the effect that deductibles will have on your costs and your future experience modification.

<u>Experience Modification</u>

Most banks have, as part of the premium calculation, a factor that is a ratio of expected losses to actual losses. This factor is known as an experience modification. Ask your agent to work with you to review your experience modification worksheet for accuracy. Check the payrolls and losses that are a part of the calculation.

A modification of 1.0 indicates that your losses are average. An experience modification of 1.2 means that your losses are higher than average. A modification of .89 is reflective of loss experience better than average. Your experience modification factor is multiplied by your gross premium. So, a 1.2 mod increases your costs by 20%.

Many banks seem to be satisfied with an experience modification that hovers around 1.0. Some commentators have said that a mod at this level is the equivalent of a school grade of C. Most would agree that this is nothing to write home about.

To objectively judge your modification, determine your "perfect" mod – the mod you would carry if you experienced no losses. (Your agent should be able to provide you with info on your perfect mod. If not, call me and let's find you a new insurance agent.) The difference between your experience modification and your perfect modification indicates the part of the modification to control.

For example, if your mod is .98 and you determine that your perfect mod is .74, you then know that .24 of your experience mod is your fault. No losses would mean a reduction in your mod of the .24. You can also use this information to determine what your losses cost you in additional premium.

Controlling your experience modification is a function of your efforts controlling your loss frequency and the severity of losses you have. It also is a function of claims management. (See this book's section on workers' compensation claims management.)

Your Perfect Mod

Your workers' compensation experience modification is the ratio of your expected losses to your actual losses. Your perfect mod is the experience modification you'd have if there were no losses on your record.

Figuring out the difference between the two tells you the impact your claims have on your premium. Contact me for a report showing your mod, your perfect mod, and the impact loss severity and frequency has on your claims – email Scott@ScottSimmonds.com

Employers' Liability

This is the second (and often ignored) part of the workers' compensation insurance policy. It covers the employer from bodily injury liability arising out of the employment relationship—but not injuries to employees.

In my career I have seen two claims in employers' liability. Neither was from banking exposures; however, they serve to illustrate the coverage.

The first was a construction risk where a wife brought lunch to her husband at a job site. On arrival at the site, she witnessed her husband falling to his death. She claimed emotional distress at seeing the accident.

The second claim was in a boatbuilding operation where a father's work clothing was contaminated with fiberglass particles. The clothing was washed in the family laundry, where the children picked up the fibers and got sick.

In the banking world, claims could come from a spouse's claim of loss of companionship or services after an employee's injury.

Typical Limits of Coverage for Employers' Liability

Each Accident $100,000

Disease—policy limit $500,000

Disease—each employee $100,000

Some umbrella insurers require higher limits of coverage:

Each Accident $500,000

Disease – policy limit $500,000

Disease – each employee $500,000

Some specialty programs and self-insured workers' compensation plans will have limits of $1,000,000 available.

Chapter 7

Umbrella Liability

The commercial umbrella liability policy provides liability coverage in addition to your general liability, auto liability, and employers' liability (part of the workers' comp policy).

> **Umbrella Coverage Example**
>
> If you have a $5,000,000 umbrella policy and an auto liability policy with $1,000,000 of coverage, the total amount of protection you have for an auto accident is $6,000,000.

Underlying Coverage

Do the limits of coverage for underlying policies meet the umbrella requirements? Each umbrella policy will outline the coverage limits for the underlying policies. Failure to meet these limits may mean a gap in coverage between the liability coverage and the umbrella.

Standard Underlying Requirements:	
Auto Liability	$1,000,000
General Liability	$1,000,000 per occurrence
	$3,000,000 aggregate
Employers' Liability	$500,000 each accident
	$500,000 Disease – policy limit
	$500,000 Disease – each employee

Concurrence of Policy Dates

Are the policy dates of your underlying policies the same as the umbrella policy? Having a single date prevents problems of missing a renewal date and issues of aggregate limits of coverage.

Mental Anguish

Are mental injury and mental anguish a part of the policy definition of bodily injury?

Multiple Liability Policies

If you have more than one general liability policy, be sure your umbrella policy applies as excess coverage over each. (While I can't think of a good reason why a bank would have more than one general liability policy, I have seen three cases recently where the bank's insurance agent had purchased separate business owners insurance policies for leased branch buildings. I can't explain why this was done—I just know I see it fairly often.)

Personal Injury Exclusions

Review the definitions and exclusions relative to personal injury. You may find additional exclusions in your umbrella policy or different definitions from those in the underlying policies. Internet marketing activities may be excluded or limited.

Review your umbrella policy exclusions. The coverage may be more restrictive than your primary policies.

Coverage Limits

The limit of umbrella liability coverage you buy for your bank will depend on the size of your bank, where you're located, and the cost of coverage. I consider $5 million to be the minimum for even the smallest bank. Get quotes at various limits of coverage so you can judge the value of higher limits.

Chapter 8

Mortgage Impairment Insurance

Mortgage impairment insurance protects the bank from errors made in the management of collateral or government guarantees that support a mortgage.

There are three parts to most policies:

<u>Mortgage Impairment</u>

This section protects your interest in a mortgage from a physical damage loss (fire, lightning, wind, etc.) as a result of "required" perils when your customer has not kept insurance in force or has not properly insured the property.

Mortgage Impairment Example

A mortgage customer allows his homeowner's insurance to lapse. Your loan department is not aware of the cancellation. The home burns, leveling the structure. Mortgage impairment insurance protects the bank's loan amount.

Most policies respond to the perils (causes of loss) required of the mortgage customer. If the loan requires "fire, extended coverage, and vandalism," then the mortgage impairment policy responds only to those perils. The insurance responds to the coverage required by your mortgage.

Some policies require that the bank track and check customer insurance policies. Some require regular notice to customers of the mortgage requirement to purchase insurance. Some don't require any form of tracking customer insurance policies, saving the bank a great deal of effort and administrative expense.

Most policies limit coverage for a set time from the date you are aware of a lapse in the insurance—usually 90 days. This allows you time to place coverage in your "forced-placed" property insurance program. (See separate section of this book for forced-placed coverage.)

Mortgagee's Errors and Omissions

Coverage for errors in the administration of escrowed insurance premiums or in the various government guarantee programs—VHA, GNMA, SBA, etc. The policy may include mistakes in determining the flood map location of the property. Failure to administer property tax payments properly for the customer also is a part of many policies.

Non-Required Perils or Balance of Perils

Supplements the perils covered by the first part of the mortgage impairment policy. Don't overlook the importance of this section. Your mortgage's required perils may not include damage by weight of ice and snow, vandalism, pipes freezing, water damage, and building collapse. Coverage can also be included here for flood and earthquake.

General Comments

- There is no universal mortgage impairment policy language. Each insurer's policy is unique, with distinctive terms and conditions.
- Be sure the perils insured are broad in nature. Consider adding coverage for flood and earthquake.
- Some insurers exclude mobile homes from coverage on the basic policy. You can purchase the coverage for an additional premium.
- Most impairment policies require that you obtain proof that insurance is in place at the time the mortgage is closed. You can do nothing that would lead a mortgage customer to believe he doesn't need to buy insurance.
- Some mortgage impairment policies require that you annually provide a written notice to customers that insurance is required as a condition of the mortgage.

- Review your policy to see if you are required to maintain proof of insurance coverage. Most policies now only require action at the time you are notified that coverage has been cancelled.

Chapter 9

Forced-Placed/Foreclosed Property Insurance

Once it has been discovered that a mortgaged property is not insured by the mortgagee, coverage must be "placed" in force by the bank.

Most bank mortgage impairment policies (see earlier section of this book) allow 90 days to place alternate coverage from the time it is discovered that an insurance policy has lapsed. Forced-placed policies are one way to insure a customer's property when the customer fails to obtain insurance. The amount of coverage is usually the amount of the outstanding loan. Banks can (in most states) charge the premium back to the customer's account.

Most forced-placed policies are on a reporting form. The insurance company charges a minimum deposit premium ($500 for a small- to medium-sized bank is not unusual), and reports of the property to be covered are made each month to the insurance company. The deposit is used up as the reports of property covered accumulate. Insurers then bill additional premium to the bank.

Be aware of the perils insured, and penalties for missed reports. Also, coverage for foreclosed properties usually can be added to most policies at a different (more costly) premium rate.

Some smaller banks are able to place the property insurance through a local agent. This tends to involve more administrative work on the bank's part, as each property will be individually underwritten by an insurer. There also may be restrictions to coverage for loss by vandalism when a property is vacant and covered by a standard policy.

Chapter 10

Lender's Single Interest Insurance Policies

Lender's single interest insurance protects the bank from loss or damage to personal property that is the collateral for loans—cars, trucks, boats, RVs, snowmobiles, and other personal property. Coverage is provided for the bank's interest and not that of the borrower.

- Be careful of potential overlap of coverage, lender's single interest with the mortgage impairment insurance on mobile homes.
- Coverage usually is included for repossessed property. Policies can include protection for title errors and omissions as well.
- Most lender single interest policies are paid for on a monthly reporting basis. The bank reports the value of secured loans and a premium is charged for the exposure.
- Coverage can include repossession expense reimbursement, mechanic's lien reimbursement,

gap/deficiency coverage, borrower deductible coverage, and vehicle location/skip reimbursement.

- Lender's Single Interest is usually sold by specialty insurers.

- Bank trade associations often have access to special programs.

Chapter 11

Unique Issues of Claims-Made Policies

Before we get into the directors' and officers' policy (D&O) or the employment practices liability policy, let's review the components of claims-made insurance.

Most casualty insurance policies (general liability, automobile, workers' compensation) pay for events that occur during the policy period. For example, an auto insurance policy will pay for an accident that occurs while the policy is in force. D&O policies, however, pay for lawsuits filed during the policy period; the wrongful act could have occurred years before. Claims-made policies respond only when a suit is filed, or when a strong threat of a suit exists.

Difference between Claims-Made and Occurrence

Claims-made policy: pays based on the date of the lawsuit.

Occurrence policy: pays based on the date of the accident or occurrence.

The downside of a claims-made policy comes if the policy is cancelled.

Example: A D&O policy is put in force January 1, 2004, and is renewed in 2005 and 2006. In 2007, however, the bank decides to end the coverage, as the premium has increased. Six months later, a letter from an attorney arrives announcing a lawsuit for discrimination in hiring that occurred in 2006. No coverage. Although the policy was in force at the time of the alleged discrimination, the policy was not in force when the suit was filed.

The solution to the above problem is the extended reporting period found in most policies (see the next paragraph).

Discovery Period/Tail/Reporting Period Issues

Claims-made policies provide protection for lawsuits and actions brought during the policy period. In the event that coverage is replaced or cancelled, protection may be desired for events that took place prior to expiration/cancellation but for which no claim has yet been filed. This is called a "tail" or "extended reporting period."

Issues to Consider:

- Can the insured buy the Extended Reporting Period (ERP) at their option or only when the insurance company cancels the policy?
- For what time period is the extension of reporting valid? You may want at least 3 years of coverage.
- What is the premium for the ERP?
- In what time frame must the insured decide to buy the ERP?

Retroactive Date

Claims-made policies respond to claims brought during the policy period as long as the occurrence (the date of the wrongful act) takes place after the "retroactive date." When changing insurance companies, it is vital to understand the new policy retro date. The use of a "tail" may be necessary if the retro date is not sufficiently in the past.

Chapter 12

Directors' and Officers' Insurance

There are no standard D&O insurance policies. Coverage provided varies widely by insurer. Each policy and proposal of coverage must be reviewed and analyzed carefully to determine the best offering based upon the needs of the financial institution.

Summary of Coverage

Bank directors and officers have a fiduciary responsibility to customers, shareholders, and the general public in all dealings. There are also regulatory issues. The purpose of directors' and officers' insurance is to protect the personal assets of the directors, officers, and employees of a financial institution from losses arising from "wrongful acts."

Each insurer has a unique definition for "wrongful act." The term generally means any actual or alleged act or omission, error, misstatement, misleading statement, neglect, or breach of duty by an "insured person" in the discharge of his/her duties with the financial institution.

"Insured persons" are (generally) any past, present or future director, officer or employee, or honorary director or trustee of the financial institution.

Losses include any amount that the insured persons are legally obligated to pay, including judgments, settlements, defense costs, pre- and post-judgment interest, and punitive damages (where insurable by law).

The primary purpose of D&O coverage is the protection of the directors and officers of the bank. Most banks indemnify the directors and officers. However, litigation without insurance can put a severe dent in the financial statements. Legal expenses can be substantial.

Unendorsed D&O policies do not provide protection for the "entity," the bank itself. Many lawsuits name one or more "insured persons" and the bank. In such a case, without entity protection, judgments, settlements, and costs of defense will be allocated by the insurer between the financial institution and the individual insured persons. If the allocation determines that 60 percent of the action was attributable to an insured person, the D&O policy (without entity coverage) would pay only 60 percent of the judgment. The balance would not be covered.

In general, courts impose on financial institutions a greater duty than they impose on individuals. This places the majority of any loss involving the entity and an insured person on the bank. There is no formula to determine the allocation of costs and awards between bank and individual.

Disputes between the insurance carrier and the bank can lead to frustration and higher attorneys' fees.

Entity protection is available through most D&O insurance companies. Carriers provide coverage by an endorsement to the D&O policy. Many carriers include extra coverage relative to entity acts, making the D&O policy a broad "errors & omissions" type of contract. Protection can be provided for:

- Securities-related suits;
- Shareholder suits;
- Lending-related suits brought by borrowers or guarantors;
- Suits brought by depositors alleging negligence with regard to any kind of forgery, unauthorized withdrawals, or any employee dishonesty;
- Suits related to electronic banking activities;
- Suits related to IRA or Keogh plan administration;
- Suits alleging breach of fiduciary duty or employee benefit plan liability;
- Suits alleging notary errors and omissions;
- Suits alleging negligence regarding investment advice;
- Suits related to data processing operations performed by the financial institution;
- Suits brought by business partners;
- Suits served against the bank by third parties wronged by business partners or scam artists, who

allege that the bank is negligent simply by virtue of being the perpetrator's depository;

- Nuisance suits initiated by those who go after the "deep pockets" of the financial institution.

D&O policies also can include protection for "employment-related practices" such as discrimination, wrongful discharge, sexual harassment and the like.

Coverage Considerations

No Standard Coverage

As there are no standard D&O policies, each policy and proposal must be evaluated on its own merits.

Claims-Made Policy

See the separate section describing claims-made policy issues.

Policy Limit

What amount of coverage is provided? What is the total amount of protection offered for the total of all claims during the covered time frame (also known as an aggregate limit)? D&O policies are "claims-made contracts." Coverage applies to any claim brought during the policy period. Multiple claims can, in effect, use up the limit of coverage.

Many factors must be considered when deciding what policy limits your institution should carry: price, terms of the policy, peer data, regulatory requirements, and capital levels.

Appendix 2 of this book includes peer data accumulated by Progressive Insurance on the coverage purchased by their customers.

Entity Coverage Included in Policy Limit

Entity coverage makes sense for most banks. However, it can dilute the limits of coverage available for true D&O claims. The bank could run out of insurance since each claim reduces the coverage available for future claims.

Having entity claims outside the basic policy limit or as a separate limit protects the bank from using up the coverage. Alternately, the bank can purchase higher limits of coverage.

Side A, B, and C

Some D&O policies break up the coverage into three sections, A, B, and C. Some just use A and B.

Side A is coverage for individual directors and officers. Side B pays for incidents where individual directors and officers are sued when indemnification of the individuals is allowed. Side C is coverage for the company (a.k.a. the bank). Some policies use the term "entity" to describe who is insured by this section.

Side A only comes into play when indemnification is not allowed. Side B claims are the most common in incidents involving individual directors and officers.

Positions Covered

All policies define "insured persons." The contract may indicate directors, officers, and employees, or some variation. Most contracts extend coverage to "past, present, and future" directors, officers, and employees.

Defense within Limit

It is common for D&O policies to include the cost of defending a claim (attorneys' fees, etc.) within the policy limit of liability. That means that the amount of coverage purchased must be enough to cover the awards and the defense costs of all claims. This can also be an issue to consider relative to occurrence limits.

Failure to Provide Insurance Exclusion

This exclusion currently exists in very few policies. In the past, insurance companies would not provide D&O coverage for claims brought by, for example, a stockholder, for a loss due to the failure of the bank to buy enough or the right kind of insurance.

Hammer Clause

This appropriately named policy provision limits the insurer's liability should the insured refuse to accept a settlement offer from the plaintiff. In many cases, the insurance policy limits the insurer's obligation to the amount of the settlement offered. Some also restrict defense costs when the insured wishes to continue the fight.

Marital Estates Extension

This coverage provides protection for the spouse of an "insured person" when suit is brought against community property or property held jointly. Coverage only applies when the actions of the "insured person" cause the claim. For example, an officer is sued over issues surrounding a loan application. The officer's spouse is also brought into the suit, as she owns the family home. The marital estates extension provides the spouse with coverage.

Non-Cancellation Endorsement

Who can cancel the policy? Can the insurance company decide they no longer want to provide coverage? Some policies allow only the insured to cancel the policy—other than for nonpayment of premium.

Note: Most policies do not guarantee premiums. An insurer may not be able to cancel your policy but may be able to triple your premiums!

Nonprofit Service

Provides protection for actions by an "insured person" arising out of his work as a board member for a nonprofit when it is considered part of his bank duties to perform such a public service. Coverage is usually excess over any insurance the nonprofit has.

Coverage Sections and Extensions

Civil Money Penalties

Provides coverage for penalties assessed by regulatory agencies against directors and officers.

Employment-Related Practices Coverage

Employment practices liability coverage can be a part of the D&O insurance or a separate policy. The protection provided includes such issues as wrongful discharge, harassment, discrimination, etc. Check the policy's definition of "wrongful employment act." Does it include only certain acts, such as sexual harassment? Or is the coverage broad, including workplace harassment, for example? Are discrimination suits brought by third parties covered? Remember that including employment practices claims in your organization's D&O policy could affect the limit of liability available for other claims.

See the separate discussion on employment practices liability policies.

Bankers Professional Liability Insurance

Some insurers use a separate coverage section of the D&O policy called Bankers Professional Liability (BPL). Coverage is provided for issues such as sales of investments, investment advice, insurance sales, and lender's liability. Some BPL policies limit coverage for professional liability suits brought by customers. Some policies require that the relationship between the bank and the party bringing suit be based on a fee relationship. Review the policy to be certain that insurers use a broad definition of a fee relationship to include any transaction where the bank receives some tangible benefit.

Fiduciary Liability

Coverage for errors and omissions in the duties prescribed by the federal law ERISA for the administration of the bank's own employee benefit plan. This also may be a separate policy.

IRA/Keogh Liability

Covers the bank against liability caused by errors or omissions while acting as administrator or trustee of IRA or HR 10/Keogh plans.

Lender Liability

Protects the financial institution against lawsuits alleging improper procedures, extension of credit, refusal to lend, or improper servicing of loans.

Remember that every directors' and officers' liability policy is unique. Read your policy!

Securities Liability

Protection for the entity against lawsuits resulting from the purchase or sale of, or the offer to purchase or sell, any securities issued by the insured.

Trust Errors & Omissions

Protects the bank from liability arising out of wrongful acts in the administration of trust accounts. The coverage may be an endorsement to the D&O policy or a separate, stand-alone policy. In any event, make sure that coverage for this protection does not erode the aggregate limit of coverage on the D&O.

Chapter 13

Employment Practices Liability Insurance

An employee claims to have been harassed by a supervisor. A teller discharged for chronic customer service complaints claims age discrimination. An unsuccessful job applicant alledges he didn't get the job because of his race. These are all liabilities included in employment-related practices insurance. The topic was touched on briefly in the D&O section, since coverage can be included in that policy. We'll go into more detail here.

Summary of Coverage

The policy is designed to address liabilities that come out of the employment relationship. Workers' compensation, issues involving unemployment insurance and ERISA are excluded.

Coverage is generally included for harassment, discrimination, wrongful discharge, failure to hire, and failure to promote.

Coverage Considerations

As there are no standard EPLI policies, each policy and proposal must be evaluated on its own merits. Here are some issues that should be considered:

Claims-Made Policy

See the separate section of this book describing claims-made policy issues.

Limit of Coverage

Most EPLI policies have a limit per occurrence and a policy limit of coverage for the total of all claims, called an aggregate limit. As claims are paid, you use up the limit of coverage available for future claims.

Defense within Limit

Most EPLI policies include the cost of defending a claim (attorneys' fees, etc.) within the policy limit of liability. The defense costs of a claim can use up your insurance. When looking for the correct limit of coverage, consider the cost of the legal system in your calculations.

Definition of Wrongful Employment Practice

Each EPLI policy will contain a definition of the wrongful acts that are included in the policy.

Here are some acts to be considered when reviewing coverage:

- Discrimination
- Negligent Hiring
- Wrongful Discharge, Evaluation, Discipline, Promotion
- Employment-Related Personal Injury (Libel or Slander)
- Sexual Harassment
- Workplace Harassment
- Failure to Hire
- Workplace Tort – Wrongful Termination, Retention, etc.

If an act is outside the definition of wrongful act, there is no coverage.

Definition of Harassment

Some policies narrowly define this coverage as "sexual harassment." A better (broader) definition is "workplace harassment" or "harassment including sexual harassment."

Special Insurance Company Provisions

Some employment practices liability insurance policies include special features. Usually these are measures to prevent losses. Insurers may provide access to a "hotline," allowing free access to experts to discuss employment actions and situations. The purpose is to give the bank access to information and opinions on issues that could lead to a claim.

Another feature offered by some insurers is a reduction in the deductible applied to a claim if the bank called an attorney prior to the termination of an employee. Some insurers provide a hotline. Others allow you to call your own attorney. Should a claim result, the deductible is reduced by half.

Chapter 14

Financial Institutions Bond

The Financial Institutions Bond covers the bank for issues of dishonesty and fraud. The bond is a first-party policy—it protects the bank against loss of the bank's assets.

Summary of Basic Coverage

The current coverage form has evolved over the years from the four basic agreements included in the standard "Form 24" used for many years. Here are the basic coverages:

Employee Dishonesty/Fidelity

Covers dishonest or fraudulent acts committed by employees acting alone or in collusion with others—embezzlement. The employee must have intended to cause the bank a loss or to obtain financial benefit.

On Premises

Protection for the loss of property resulting from robbery; burglary; misplacement; mysterious, unexplainable disappearance; theft; false pretenses; or larceny. The property stolen can be owned by the bank, a customer, or an employee.

In Transit

Loss of property resulting directly from robbery, larceny, theft, misplacement while the property is in transit away from the bank. Property must be in the custody of a person acting as a messenger of the bank or a transportation company. Money, gems, jewelry, or precious metals being transported by a transportation company must be in an armored vehicle.

Money transported by a courier (not an armored car) is not covered.

Counterfeit Currency

Loss resulting from the good faith receipt by the bank of counterfeit money. Be sure the definition of "money" includes all currency of foreign governments.

Summary of Optional Coverage

Here are the additional coverages that have become standard in most policies:

Agents Coverage

Amends the policy definition of employee to include persons, partnerships or corporations (such as conveyancers, collectors of rents or savings from persons making systematic deposits with the insured; but excluding servicing contractors, managers of real property, data processing organizations, and independent software contractors), duly elected or appointed by the bank to serve as its agent.

Audit and Claims Expense

Covers reasonable expenses incurred and paid by the bank for audits or examinations required by state or federal regulators when the audits are conducted either by such authorities or by independent accountants due to the discovery of any valid and collectible loss under employee dishonesty/fidelity coverage.

Automated Teller Machines

Loss of property located within an ATM machine including damage to the machine itself caused by burglary, robbery, or attempted burglary or robbery. Some policies limit coverage to ATMs that are a part of a bank building.

Check Kiting Fraud

Covers loss resulting directly from checks that are finally not paid because of a check kiting fraud established against the bank.

Computer Systems Fraud

Covers loss from a fraudulent entry of electronic data or computer program within a covered computer system.

Data Processing Service Operations

Covers loss sustained by a customer of the bank, resulting directly from a fraudulent entry of electronic data or computer program into, or change of electronic data or program within a computer system covered by the policy, or entry or change of electronic data during electronic transmission or physical transit from the bank to its client, and for which loss the insured is legally liable to the client as a provider of data processing services.

Debit Card Coverage

Provides coverage for loss resulting directly from the fraudulent use of a debit card to obtain cash or pay for products or services by gaining access to an electronic payment device, provided that such device, as part of the transaction, electronically verifies the customer's available funds in the customer's depository account at the insured's bank.

Destruction of Data or Programs by Hacker

Covers loss resulting directly from the malicious destruction of, or damage to computer programs owned by the bank, or for which the bank is legally liable, while stored within a computer system covered under the terms of the computer systems fraud coverage section. Protection is usually included for the cost of duplicating damaged or destroyed data or computer programs from backup sources.

If the computer programs cannot be duplicated from a backup, the insurance company will pay the additional costs to restore damaged or destroyed data.

Destruction of Data or Programs by Virus

Covers loss from the malicious destruction of, or damage to, electronic or computer programs owned by the bank, or for which the bank is legally liable, while stored within a computer system. Protection is usually included for the cost of duplicating damaged or destroyed data or computer programs from backup sources, or the additional costs of restoring the damaged data.

Forgery/Unauthorized Signature

Provides protection against a loss caused by an unauthorized signature; or the alteration of a negotiable instrument, including a counterfeit check, letter of acceptance, withdrawal order, certificate of deposit, letter of credit, or receipt of the withdrawal of property. This coverage usually does not apply to an evidence of debt.

Fraudulent Mortgages

Covers loss through the bank having, in good faith, acted upon any real property mortgages or similar instruments which prove to be defective by reason of the signature on such instruments having been obtained by trick or false pretenses.

Indemnity for Injury or Death of Directors or Employees

Covers payments made to directors or employees who were injured or whose death was caused by any person who is committing or attempting to commit any act of larceny, theft, robbery, or burglary.

Kidnap-Ransom-Extortion

Covers the loss of money surrendered and expenses incurred as a result of:

1) the actual or alleged kidnapping of an insured person;

2) a threat to kill, injure, or kidnap an insured person;

3) a threat to cause physical damage to and/or contaminate or pollute the insured's property;

4) a threat to disseminate, divulge or utilize any confidential, private or secret information unique to the insured's business, which is protected by physical or electronic controls;

5) a threat to alter, adulterate, or destroy any of the insured's computer programs by introducing into the insured's computer systems, instructions or data which are not authorized by the insured.

Securities

Covers losses resulting from extending credit on the faith of stock certificates, documents of title, deeds, mortgages, certificates of title, corporate or personal guarantees, evidences of debt, and security agreements that are forged, altered, counterfeited, lost, or stolen. The bank must have relied in good faith upon an original instrument. The document must have been in the physical possession of the bank, its correspondent, or representative.

Servicing Contractors

Extends coverage for loss resulting from dishonest acts of a person or organization that collects and records payments on real estate mortgage or home improvement loans, or a manager of real property under the control of the insured.

Stop Payment or Wrongful Dishonor

Provides coverage for loss that the insured is legally liable to pay due to the insured's:

1) failure to comply with a customer's request to stop payment on a negotiable instrument;
2) refusing to pay a negotiable instrument; and
3) failure to give proper notice of dishonor.

Telefacsimile Transfer Fraud

Covers loss resulting directly from the bank having, in good faith, transferred or delivered funds, certificated securities or uncertificated securities through a computer system covered under the terms of the computer systems fraud coverage section, in reliance upon a fraudulent instruction received through a telefacsimile device.

Trading Loss

The employee dishonesty coverage in many bonds excludes losses involving trading (any purchase, exchange or sale transaction). Trading loss coverage buys back the exclusion. Therefore, coverage is provided for a loss caused by an employee's fraudulent trades.

Transit Cash Letter Rider

Cash letters are usually covered within the "in transit" coverage. Some insurers offer coverage that extends the protection by eliminating the deductible, providing reimbursement for reproduction costs, and extending coverage beyond the final destination of the cash letter to the financial institution upon which an item was drawn. Insurers usually require that the front and back of each item placed in the cash letter be photocopied.

Voice-Initiated Transfer Fraud

This coverage is available only in conjunction with computer systems fraud coverage. Provides the bank with protection for loss resulting directly from the insured having, in good faith, transferred funds from a customer's account through a computer system covered under the terms of the computer systems fraud section, in reliance upon a fraudulent voice instruction transmitted by telephone.

Voice Computer System Fraud

Covers loss resulting directly from toll call charges incurred due to the fraudulent use or fraudulent manipulation of an account code or systems password required to obtain access to the insured's voice computer system.

Chapter 15

Combination Safe Depository

Some insurers provide coverage for a safe depository as a separate policy. Others include it in the bond. The policy provides coverage for all sums the bank is legally liable to pay because of the loss, damage, or destruction of a customer's property from a safe depository. Some policies allow for the exclusion of money at a reduced premium.

Safe depository coverage can be written in two broad ways:

- Liability of Depository – covers loss that the insured shall become legally obligated to pay by reason of liability for loss of customers' property.

- Loss of Customers' Property – covers loss of customers' property by burglary or robbery, or attempt thereat, or for damage to or destruction of customers' property regardless of the liability of the bank.

Determining the limits of safe depository coverage that your bank needs is a tough call. What is the largest exposure to loss you have at any of your locations? What do your customers have stored in their boxes? Both are unanswerable questions. Start at $1,000,000 and get quotes for more.

Chapter 16

E-Banking Risk Coverage

The currently available bond and D&O policies do a great job of taking care of the primary (and greatest loss potential) exposures that come with Internet banking. Computer fraud, data destruction by hacker, extortion, and destruction by virus are all part of most Financial Institutions Bonds.

That being said, some insurers have designed special forms to provide supplemental coverage. Each insurance carrier's form is unique and must be studied carefully. Here are some common coverage considerations:

<u>Policy Aggregate</u>

The total amount of payments the insurer will make; the combination of all coverage sections and claims.

Business Income Loss

Provides protection from the loss of income that results from a bank's e-banking system being inoperable.

Dependent Business

Provides loss of business income protection for the loss of services provided to you by others for Web services, e-banking support, and the like.

Intellectual Property

Indemnifies the bank from the liability presented for use of the intellectual property of others on a Web site or e-banking facility. Can include copyright infringement, theft of ideas, and trademark misuse.

Public Relations

Provides payment for the use of public relations firms and advertising to mitigate the damage to public perception should an e-banking breach occur.

Loss Event Liability

Broad coverage for liability that arises out of any unauthorized use of, or unauthorized access to, electronic data or software within your covered electronic business systems.

Coverage is also included for:

- malicious, subversive or unauthorized introduction of any computer code, program or other data into, or attack upon, the bank's covered electronic business systems, causing the alteration, distortion, deletion, destruction, degradation, corruption, malfunction, compromise or loss of access to the bank's computer systems;

- computer theft, extortion, or any unintentional act, mistake, error or omission made by your employees or subcontractors, in the course of their duties, in connection with the creation, development, modification or implementation of any set of related instructions to direct the operations and functions of your covered computer systems.

A Few Thoughts on E-Banking Insurance

I am not a big fan of the current crop of e-banking insurance policies. While these policies have their place, I question the value of the insurance contracts for most community banks, given the breadth of coverage available in the bond, directors' & officers', and package policies.

Is the premium spent on these policies better used increasing the limit of coverage in the bond, D&O, or umbrella liability?

Review the e-banking forms offered by your insurance company. Discuss the specific coverage included in your traditional insurance program.

Ask what gaps exist in the bond for a hacker getting account numbers or moving funds between accounts. Ask what liability issues presented by e-banking are not addressed by the general liability or directors' & officers' insurance.

Consider what your true loss of business income would be if your e-banking system were to go down for a week or two.

To be clear, I'm not saying there is no need for this policy. I'm saying that the coverage provided may not be as valuable as other protections.

Last point, this is a quickly evolving part of bank insurance. Every renewal should be reviewed carefully for these issues.

Chapter 17

Terrorism Insurance

Terrorism is an issue that can affect clients in all lines of insurance.

The U.S. Congress has required that insurers provide limited terrorism coverage as an option on most insurance policies. The Terrorism Risk Insurance Act of 2002 (TRIA) provides protection for terrorist acts that fall within certain parameters. Here is some general information about TRIA:

- TRIA is a federal program with mandatory participation (by insurance companies).
- Covers only foreign-led attacks on U.S. property that cause at least $100 million in damages (2007).
- Feds pay for 85% of any losses above an insurance company's deductible.
- Insurer of record is responsible for 15% of any losses after a 20% deductible.
- Annual losses covered by the program are capped at $100 billion.

In most states, insurers exclude all terrorism then add back TRIA coverage if the client wants the protection.

While TRIA may seem fairly broad, the coverage is actually quite restrictive. For example, an act of domestic terrorism by an abortion-rights group or fanatical religious organization would be excluded by most policies and would not be included under TRIA. The Oklahoma City bombing would not be covered by TRIA. Also, a "minor" event (under $100 million) where a biological agent was mailed to a bank would be excluded by the policy and not covered by TRIA.

Insurers offer TRIA quotes at policy inception and renewal. The exception is workers' compensation, where TRIA coverage is automatically included.

I suggest that banks ask their insurance broker to quote "full" terrorism coverage. You can then determine the value of the coverage versus the standard offered TRIA protection.

Chapter 18

Overview – How to Bid Your Insurance

It is almost an automatic part of the insurance transaction for most banks. Each year premiums slowly increase (sometimes not so slowly). Experience shows that without competitive bidding, your insurance premium will go up.

There are complications. Some banks want to deal with a specific agent in town, usually a customer or board member. Perhaps you wish to use two agents, or more.

My intent in this section isn't to tell you there is only one way to bid your coverage. I understand (and have dealt with) the political and business issues in selecting agents. My purpose in this section is to give you tools to select the agents and insurers you deal with on a qualitative basis.

Here are some truths I have found in my work for community banks:

- Having two agents bid for your coverage in a competitive process will get you the absolute best combination of coverage and price. You then have to interpret the results of the process.

- Having one agent bid the bank's coverage within their own fleet of insurers can provide some of the benefits of a bid while keeping the same agent.

- Selecting an agent using an orderly process can result in a better insurance program at a better price.

Chapter 19

To Bid or Not to Bid

There are two ways to search for alternatives to your current agent and insurer. You can pick a few agents and have them submit competitive bids. Such is the traditional bid process—multiple agents and multiple quotes.

The second option is to select one agent to obtain quotes from multiple insurers, called agent selection. This may happen using your current agent or you can review the services of multiple agents and select the one you feel best meets your bank's needs. Once you select the agent, he or she goes to work for you.

Competitive Bid Process Steps

Step 1 Select agents that you believe may be able to handle your account.

Step 2 Have agents complete an information questionnaire.

Step 3 Select participating agents.

Step 4 Provide basic information about your business to the participating agents and ask them for listings of proposed insurers.

Step 5 Assign the insurers each agent will be able to access.

Step 6 Provide full bid specifications and claim data to the participating agents.

Step 7 Agents interview you and gather additional information they need to provide bids.

Step 8 Agents present proposals. You review proposals and select the program you believe is best.

Step 9 Successful agent implements the program.

Agent Selection Process Steps

Step 1 Select participating agents.

Step 2 Agents complete information questionnaire.

Step 3 Select participating agents to interview.

Step 4 Interview the successful agents.

Step 5 Review proposals and select the agent you believe is best.

Step 6 Successful agent implements the program, gathers information, accesses insurance companies, and follows through on obtaining proposals.

Comparative Points

Advantages and disadvantages need to be considered in how you will go about your review of your insurance relationships:

Competitive Bid Process	Agent Selection Process
The process is time consuming, as you must educate multiple agents about your bank.	Less time commitment in educating multiple agents about your business.
Usually results in a lower price due to competition.	No conflicts on the assignment of insurance companies.
You'll get multiple opinions as to exposures and coverage needed—a good thing.	Broker has full access to the marketplace, allowing for the use of several insurance companies within the proposed program.
Trying to compare the coverage offered by more than one agent may result in confusion—different coverage limits, terms, and conditions. Each agent will usually claim his program is the best.	There is a chance that the successful agent may not be as aggressive on pricing as in a full competitive bid situation.

Timing

While you can go through the agent selection process at any time during the year, in most cases you'll want the decision in place in time to prepare for the renewal. Your decision should be made with at least 90 days' lead time to program renewal. Obviously, the bid process is performed close to the policy renewal dates.

Sample Time Line – Bid Process:

Select prospective agents for initial round	130 days prior to renewal
Phone calls to prospective agents	125 days prior
Send out questionnaires to agents	120 days prior
Questionnaires due from agents	115 days prior
Notify selected agents for actual bid	110 days prior
Assign insurance companies to selected agents	105 days prior
Send bid specifications	100 days prior
Agent information-gathering meetings	90–100 days prior
Bids due	21 days prior
Agent selection and start of agent's work to assume your account	10 days prior
Program renewal	Renewal

Sample Time Line – Agent Selection Process:

Select prospective agents	150 days prior to renewal
Phone calls to prospective agents	145 days prior
Send out questionnaires to agents	140 days prior
Questionnaires due from agents	125 days prior
Notify selected agents	118 days prior
Pre-interview meetings for agents who want more information	119–103 days prior
Interviews/presentations by agents	104 days prior
Agent selection and start of agent's work to assume your account	90 days prior
Program renewal	Renewal

How to Find the Right Agents for the Process

Regardless of whether you bid your insurance or use the agent selection process, you start by identifying prospective agents. Here are some general thoughts:

- Rarely do I recommend excluding your current insurance agent from the process.
- Talk to business people in your area whom you respect. Find out who their agent is—the agent and the agency.
- Call your state banker's association. Find out what agents are sponsored by the association. What agents are members?
- Consider regional agencies from surrounding cities.

Once you build a list of five to ten firms, get on the phone. Call the agent (or agency) and tell him your situation. You may have to leave a message on voice mail. Cross any agent off your list who does not call you back in one business day. (By the way, my personal standard is 90 minutes for a call-back. It's a promise I make to all my clients—phone calls returned in 90 minutes—email returned in 24 hours.)

Think of the first phone call as speed dating. You're going to spent ten minutes talking with the agent about what you're doing. You want a quick impression of whether there is a reason to pursue the relationship. After the phone conversation, decide if the agent is someone you would like to learn more about. If so, put him or her on your list of potential agents and move on in your process.

If you plan to utilize the Agent Selection Process, go to Chapter 20.

If you plan to use a Bid Process with several agents, go to Chapter 21.

Chapter 20

Agent Selection Process

Quick review, in case you jumped to this section. There are two ways to pick an insurance agent—bid or agent selection process. Go to Chapter 19 for a review of the advantages of both approaches.

If you plan to use a Bid Process with several agents, go to Chapter 21.

Agent Qualification Questionnaire Form

Using the previous section of this book, you should have a list of potential agents—more than four but fewer than ten. Five usually works quite well.

Send each agent the Agent Qualification Questionnaire Form included in Appendix 3.

Email me at Scott@ScottSimmonds.com **to receive the Agent Qualification Questionnaire Form in Microsoft Word format. You'll save time and effort.**

The purpose of the questionnaire is to learn more about the agents and agencies so you can move toward your final selection. Customize the document with your own information. Areas of customization are indicated by "<" and ">" marks.

Complete the "About Us" section, giving the agent an idea of who you are and what you do. Give the agents information about your business. You need to share some data here—asset size, number of employees, payroll, etc.

Send the agent your customized form as a word processing document attached to an email. This will make it easier for the agent to respond.

Agents will respond by email, fax, and mail. Some will want to meet with you prior to completing the form. I usually put a meeting off until after the forms are returned. The form is designed to give you a true feel for the agency. Can they follow instructions? Do they meet deadlines? Also, the form doesn't require much effort on the agent's part. Some brokers have a form they have used for other projects. As long as I get the information I want about the agency, I don't get too clutched about the format the agents use to respond.

Selecting Agents for the Next Step – Presentations

The form will help you decide who is qualified to go the next step, the presentation. Using the completed questionnaires, select the three agents who most clearly meet your needs. Review their experience in your type of business. How did they answer the questions? Do they seem to focus on value to you? Does it appear that their service will be responsive?

Call the successful agents to set up a presentation meeting. Be sure to call those agents who completed a questionnaire but were not selected. They put effort into the first phase of this project and deserve the courtesy of a call.

Your presentation meetings should all be held on the same day. Tell each agent he or she has 30 minutes. Schedule the presentations 45 minutes apart. This gives you some time to discuss each presentation with other members of your team and builds in time for presentations running a bit longer. Don't put off calling the agents who were not invited to make presentations. Procrastination here only will make the call tougher.

Pre-Presentation Meetings

Some agents will want to meet with you before they make their presentation. They'll want to get to know you and your business. Frankly, it's the good agents who will ask for such a meeting. I don't ask the agents for a meeting. I let them come up with the idea. Remember, you're trying to get into the agent's heads to see how interested they are in your business. What they don't do may be as important as what they do.

Plan to spend about 60 minutes with an agent in a pre-presentation meeting. Don't let the agent talk a great deal about themselves or their agency. The purpose of the meeting is for the agent to get to know you so he can do a great job in his presentation.

Agents' Presentations

In most cases, you'll want to include several of your key people in the sessions. Depending on the size and structure of your bank, your corporate officers, and human resources managers may be involved.

Some call these agent presentations "dog and pony shows." It's the agent's opportunity to show off his or her qualifications and expertise. Different agents take different approaches to the presentation. Some will bore you with an overview of the history of their agency or will give a live version of their résumé. Good agents will focus on the value they will provide you as your insurance agent. The best will provide you with a case study as an example of how they serve clients.

The presentation meeting is the agency's opportunity to tell their story. From that meeting you will select the right agency.

At the conclusion of the presentation, have questions prepared to ask all the prospective agents. Here are some examples:

- Describe a situation where you provided exceptional client service.
- We are also interviewing the ABC Agency and folks from DEF Insurance. Why should we pick you?
- Tell me about a recent situation where you lost a client.
- Describe your service team and how a request for a certificate of insurance will be handled.
- What is your process for handling a small claim?

Some questions need to be asked of each agency. You will want to compare answers by each participant:

- Will you provide us with an annual account review? When in the year will this take place?
- How will you ensure that we have renewal quotes at least 21 days before our renewal?
- What claims management services will you provide?
- What loss control services will you provide?

You're trying to get the agent talking about his or her service and approach to the business. You want the person who will be working on your account to talk. In many cases, a supervisor or principal of the agency will attend the meeting. Don't let the boss hog-the-show. You want to hear from the people who will be working on a day-to-day basis on your account, the service reps.

I try to get the team off their scripts so I can have a conversation. Ask probing questions that cause the presenters to think and speak outside of their comfort zone. These people will have millions of dollars of your assets in their care. You want sharp people on your team.

After the Presentation

On occasion, the choice of agents is easy. One agency may be the clear winner. Don't jump too fast. Pick your top two agents and ask each for a one-page, written service plan for the first year he or she will be handling your account. Explain that the choice is very difficult and that you need a bit more information.

Depending on geography, I sometimes meet the agents at their office. It gives me a chance to learn more about the agency and its culture.

The Decision

After the questionnaire, the presentation, and the written service plan, you should have a good idea with whom you'd like to work.

If you're having trouble with the decision, here are a few questions to ask yourself:

- Which agency would I like in my corner if I were in a claim dispute with my insurance company?
- Which agent seemed to be the most comfortable with the banking industry and the unique exposures presented?
- If your attorney had a question about your insurance coverage, which agent would you be most confident would provide accurate information and assistance?
- If my administrative center were destroyed by a fire, which agent would I want on my team?

Notify the successful agent and those who were not selected.

In your conversation with the successful agent, you should reiterate your intent to hold the successful agent to the service schedule he or she provided you. You expect that claims will be managed effectively and that the renewal quotations will be timely. This is the time to be clear on expectations.

Chapter 21

Bidding Your Insurance

Here is a quick review, just in case you jumped right to this section. There are two ways to pick an insurance agent—bid or agent selection process. Go to Chapter 19 for a review of the advantages of both approaches.

If you plan to use an Agent Selection Process, go to Chapter 20.

The insurance bid process is a complicated and time-consuming undertaking for most banks. It should not be entered into lightly. Many businesses have fallen into a program of bidding insurance every three or four years. If you have bid your insurance more than twice in the past six years without changing agents, the marketplace may not be thrilled with seeing you again.

Bidding is an intense process for the insurance agents and companies too. In 85 percent of all bids, the insured party ends up staying with the current insurance agent and insurance company. Many agents are leery of "practice bidding." Be honest with yourself: if another agent comes to you with a better program at a lower price, are you prepared to fire your current agent? If not, rethink bidding.

Agent Qualification Questionnaire Form

As with the agent selection process, the first step is to build a list of several potential agents. See the information in Chapter 19 to build that list. You want more than four agents but fewer than ten. Five works quite well.

Send each agent the Agent Qualification Questionnaire Form found in Appendix 3.

Email me to receive the Agent Qualification Questionnaire Form in Microsoft Word format – Scott@ScottSimmonds.com. You'll save time and effort.

The purpose of the questionnaire is to learn more about the agent and agency. Customize the document with your own information. Areas of customization are indicated by “<" and ">" marks.

You complete the”About Us" section, giving the agent information on your bank and your subsidiaries. You need to share some data here—asset size, number of employees, payroll, etc.

Send the agents your customized form as a word processing document attached to an email. This will make it easier for the agent to respond.

Agents will respond by email, fax, and mail. Some will want to meet with you prior to completing the form. I usually put any meeting off until after the forms are returned. The form is designed to give you a true feel for the agency. Can they follow instructions? Do they meet deadlines? Also, it doesn't require much effort on the agent's part. At times, brokers have a form they have used for other business owners. As long as I get the information I want about the agency, I don't get too clutched about the format the agents use to respond.

<u>Selecting Agents for the Next Step – Bid Process</u>

The form will help you decide who is qualified to go to the next step, the bid process. Using the completed questionnaires, select no more than three agents who most clearly meet your needs. Review their experience in the financial services business. Do they work with other banks?

How did they answer the questions? Do they seem to focus on value? Does it appear that their service will be responsive?

Your current agent will almost always be one of the two or three agents you pick. If you are definitely going to change brokers, fire your current agent now. Don't pretend you're happy with the service you're getting if you're not. You should have had conversations with your agent in the past if you are truly unhappy. If you plan to fire your agent, go ahead. It's never easy. It will only be harder later. Waiting may mess up the bid process, too.

Market Selection

Now that you have your agents selected, you must assign insurance companies to each agent.

In property and casualty insurance, carriers limit agents' access. If Agent A contacts Podunk Insurance Company, no other insurance agent will be able to get a quote from Podunk. This process is called market blocking—only one agent has access to an insurer. Other agents are blocked unless they get a broker of record letter signed by the insurance buyer. The broker of record letter moves the authority and access from the first agent to the agent in possession of the letter. The first agent loses access.

Confused? It's understandable! It's a confusing process. I think the whole thing is anticompetitive and wrong. I've been fighting it for 20 years. It is a tradition that protects sloppy agents at the expense of quality. It is, however, the system we have to work with in most states.

Ask the agents you have selected to submit a list of insurance companies they wish to use on your account. They should provide you the list ranked in order of preference.

When each agent submits his or her list, complete the following matrix with the agents' selections. Note: Your current agent will be using your current insurer—that automatically becomes his or her 1st choice.

	Current Agent	**Agent A**	**Agent B**
1st Choice	Current Insurer		
2nd Choice			
3rd Choice			
4th Choice			
5th Choice			
6th Choice			

Are there overlaps with the other agents and your current agent? This may be your chance to narrow down further your choice of agents.

Whenever possible I recommend that you bid with only two agents—your current agent and the strongest competitor.

Having three agents may force you to split up the markets too thinly.

By the way, the market selection process is the single toughest part of the bid process. Assign markets improperly and you may end up hurting the outcome of the bids. At times, you may have to discuss the issues with the participating agents. If one insurance company is the top choice of each agent, consider calling each agent and having them make the case for that insurer.

Frankly, in a three-agent bid situation, someone always ends up being ticked off at the assignments. It is possible that one agent will pull out at this point if he feels he cannot get a fair shot at the business with the markets assigned to him. I never held such a move against an agent. His time is valuable too.

Bid Specifications

You're going to have to put together information on your current insurance program along with claims information and underwriting information. Ask your current agent to help with this process. Most will help you. It may be a touchy subject. Some agents don't want to help the competition. Take the stand that this is part of an agent's job. Failure to cooperate here will be viewed negatively at decision time.

It is possible for each participating agent to build his own information. This will mean a great deal more time for you. Push your agent to cooperate.

Bid specs should include:

- Schedule of all vehicles, mobile equipment, buildings, and other property to be insured. No value is necessary for vehicles. Mobile equipment should show market values (actual cash value). Buildings and personal property should show replacement cost values;

- Five years of insurer loss runs (your current agent can provide these to you);

- Workers' compensation experience modification worksheets for the upcoming year and the current policy period;

- General liability premium basis (payroll, sales, square footage) based upon the current policy (available from your agent), updated for what is expected in the policy period being quoted;

- Your bank's marketing materials, web site address, sample brochures, and the like;

- Copy of your employee handbook;

- Applications from your current insurer for directors and officers, bond, and e-banking insurance coverage. (Most insurers quoting coverage will work from your current insurance company's applications.)

- Other information that may help underwriters to see the bank in a positive light.

Once the bid packet is put together, get it out to the agents. Agents need the bid specs at least 100 days before the renewal date.

Review the information in Chapter 19 regarding the timing of this process. Be clear when the bids are due. Specify that bids are due at noon on a specific date at a specific place. Events sometimes conspire, making it difficult for an agent to get bids in on time. You will have to decide if you will allow late bid presentations.

Should You Tell Everyone Your Current Premiums?

Obviously there are two schools of thought—tell and don't tell. Those in favor of "don't tell" say it keeps everyone on their toes. Everyone, that is, except your current agent. It's an advantage to your current agent to have the competing agents in the dark over your premiums. It's not a fair advantage.

I say "tell." In my bid specifications I include information on the current premiums by line of coverage. To me, this puts everyone on the same level. Everyone knows the current premiums. Nobody knows the proposed premiums.

Other Rules of the Game

Another issue you will have to deal with in a bid is: Will your current agent get the last shot at your business? It is a common practice for insurance buyers to give their current agent a last chance to match pricing of the competitors.

The logic goes like this. "We have done business together for a long time. My agent has done a great job and deserves every opportunity to keep our business."

First, if this is how you look at your agent, why are you bidding your insurance? Don't put the other agents through the exercise of bidding if, at the end of the process, your current agent is going to get the last chance to hit a stationary target.

The bid process should be fair and up front. If, at the end of the process, you plan to give your current agent the advantage of a second chance, you should reconsider going through the bid procedure.

Be clear and up front on how the bid is going to be handled. If your current agent gets a second chance, you should tell the other agents at the beginning of the process. Give them a chance to walk away before they invest 20 to 50 hours on your bid process.

To me, the only fair bid is a bid that is decided based on the proposals presented. Notice I didn't say that the best price wins. You should make your decision on services, coverage, and price.

Sample Bid Rules:

We promise to deal openly and fairly with all agents and insurance companies.

Problems rarely "take care of themselves." If you have a concern, issue, or problem, bring it up sooner rather than later.

Your proposals are confidential. We believe that an insurance marketplace that is fair and up front is in everyone's best interest. We will never reveal or share any competitive information you provide with any other agent or company prior to receiving their proposal.

In a bidding process we allow the competing agent to review "current" policies and pricing. We believe that this puts everyone on an even playing field. Everyone knows the current year's price. Nobody knows the bidding price when they submit proposals.

We do not give "second chances" in bids or proposals. We expect your best work up front. Discrepancies will be addressed without revealing any other participant's position.

We set deadlines in an effort to make the process work better for us. If you are going to miss a deadline, we are better off knowing as soon as possible.

Any proposal you provide will be reviewed on the basis of coverage, price, and services offered. We are under no obligation to purchase insurance based on price alone.

The information we provide you is accurate to the best of our knowledge.

Information Meetings

Encourage participating agents to meet with you to gather information needed for the bid. It is also your chance to get to know the agent. Good agents will request the meeting. They will want to spend some time with you and the other decision makers.

This is the agent's chance to learn about you. You also have the opportunity to see how the agent thinks and how he approaches the business. Competing agents may request different information or additional documents. Do your best to comply. I would urge you not to tell other agents (or your current agent) what info was requested by competitors. Exposure identification is an important part of what an agent is expected to do. Tipping the hand of one agent hurts the competitive process.

Don't play favorites with agents. If you're going to do that, why involve the other agents?

Bid Presentation

In the beginning of the bid process, you gave each agent a deadline. Allow agents to present bids in any format they wish. Some will email, some will mail, and some will present in person. Here's another opportunity to learn about how the agent approaches the business.

Comparing Bids

Now comes the hard part. You have to compare the different proposals. I use two tools. One is objective. The other is subjective.

For coverage comparison, I find a matrix is useful. Make a chart with columns for each bid. Down the left side, list coverage limits and issues. A sample of a form I use is included in Appendix 4. You can also use the various proposals for information on issues you should consider.

If you're having trouble with the decision, here are a few subjective questions to ask yourself:

- Which agency would I like in my corner if there were a claim dispute with my insurance company?
- Which agent seemed to be the most comfortable with the banking industry and the unique exposures our bank presents?
- If my attorney had a question about my insurance coverage, which agent would I be most confident would provide accurate information and assistance?
- If my administrative center were destroyed by a fire, which agent would I want on my team?

After Bid Interview

In cases where you are still undecided, it may be helpful to interview the agents again. Here are some general tips:

- Don't divulge the other agents' pricing.
- Don't allow the agents to amend their price.
- What coverage is included in one proposal but absent from another? Ask the agents why there is a

difference. "Bill, you didn't include coverage for business income. Any reason why? Your competition included the coverage."

- Affirm the service schedule that the agent promised. Will there be annual reviews or will you meet quarterly?

Bid Ethics

The bid process is filled with opportunities for misunderstanding and abuse. As I've stated before, industry-wide, 85 percent of all insurance bids result in the incumbent agent and insurer retaining the business. Many agents are no longer bidding insurance coverage because of the odds against them. Many choose to compete only on a broker/agent selection basis.

Here are some general thoughts about bidding:

- Treat all agents the same. Don't play favorites.
- Promise the competing agents that the current agent will not get a "last shot" at the bid.
- Be up front with each agent about your process and approach. Nobody can claim foul if the rules are spelled out ahead of time.

Chapter 22

Property Claims Management Help

The most common bank insurance claim is for damage to buildings or business property.

- Vandals paint graffiti on the side of one of your branch offices.
- A customer's vehicle hits the overhang on your drive-up window.
- An electrical circuit overheats, causing a fire at your administrative center.
- A windstorm damages the roof of your main office.

Should You Turn the Claim In?

In a prior section, I discussed the use of deductibles to reduce premiums. A high deductible means that small claims will not be insured. Your insurer will want you to report all incidents that damage your property. I recommend to my clients a more conservative approach: Don't report small property claims.

Insurers review a risk's (your bank's) claim frequency when determining premiums. Many small property claims will cause premiums to rise. Protect your bank by paying small claims without reporting them to the insurance company. (Always report workers' compensation, liability, and auto claims.)

The above being said, once you decide to move forward without your insurer, you will have a very difficult time getting the insurance company involved two months later when you find that the damage is more extensive than you originally thought. Use caution.

Protect the Property from Further Loss

You are responsible for the protection of your property after a loss. If a windstorm damages your roof, call a contractor for temporary repairs. If a fire has destroyed a part of your building, protect the rest of the building from damage by weather or thieves. Perhaps temporary repairs are in order. Perhaps you need to hire a security firm. Move undamaged property to a safe location for storage. Save receipts for what you spend and submit them to your insurance company for reimbursement. Do not make permanent repairs without first consulting your agent. Unauthorized permanent repairs may not be reimbursed.

Contact Your Insurance Agent As Quickly As Possible

Once you decide to involve your insurer, quickly inform them of your loss. In smaller claims, the adjuster will contact you by phone. Larger claims will involve regular visits from the adjuster.

Document the Damage

Take pictures of the damage. Save newspaper articles. Damaged property should not be discarded before you are given permission by your insurance company.

Document Your Expenses

Most bank insurance programs will include coverage for extra expenses you incur to get back into operation quickly. Advertisements of temporary locations, refitting another location to accommodate displaced employees, and increased cost of operations are all a part of your extra expense loss.

Document All Activity

Every conversation with the insurance company adjuster should be documented and confirmed. If you're asked to get estimates and told you can remove the rubble, send an email to the adjuster (with a copy to your agent) confirming that you will be contacting contractors and will have the rubble removed.

Act as if you are the project manager and the adjuster is a key part of the team. Work together. If things move in a direction you are not comfortable with, immediately involve your agent.

All Claims Adjustments Are Negotiations

The insurance policy outlines the coverage provided. Rarely are property claims handled 100 percent as the policy intended. You may want to add a third floor to the building that will replace the damaged structure. Perhaps you will not occupy the building as a branch but will use it as an administrative office. Perhaps you will not rebuild the building at all.

Work with the adjuster through the negotiations of your insurance claim. Bring your agent into the picture. Perhaps other advisors such as consultants, contractors, and lawyers will provide input.

Involve Your Agent in the Process

While most agents don't deal directly with claims, most will step in when there is a problem. Helping you with the process is a part of their job. Use their resources.

Chapter 23

Liability Claims Management Help

Report all accidents involving injuries or damage to property owned by others to your insurance company as soon as possible.

Train your branch staff to respond to slip and fall accidents and to report the incidents to your insurer. If you want a central reporting structure, make sure claims reports to the insurers are not delayed in the process.

In the banking world the most common general liability claim is a slip and fall accident. Parking lots, lobbies, and drive-through teller areas are where most general liability claims occur.

Document the Accident

As soon as you (or your people) are aware of an accident where a customer or member of the public is hurt, the report should be sent to the insurance company. Take pictures of the location of the accident as soon as possible. (All your locations should have a camera. Disposable cameras work well for documentation purposes.) Document the conditions that existed. Get contact info of all injured people and witnesses.

Correct any hazards that caused the accident.

Follow Up with Adjusters

Liability claims can take months to resolve. Contact the insurance company adjuster every few months to learn the status.

Chapter 24

Automobile Claims Management Help

Report all auto accidents involving injuries or damage to property owned by others to your insurance company as soon as possible—from the accident scene, if it's practical. Fast reporting is vital when there are serious injuries. In some cases, your insurer will dispatch a rapid response adjuster to the scene.

Train your employees on the importance of rapid reporting. If you want a central reporting structure, make sure claims reports to the insurers are not delayed in the process.

Auto accidents are the area of greatest liability exposure for large losses in the banking world. Any employee driving on bank business (conferences, educational seminars, chamber of commerce events, sales calls, etc.) can lead to bank liability for an accident.

Document the Accident

Take pictures of the location of the accident as soon as possible. (All bank vehicles should have a camera in an emergency kit along with the phone numbers of your insurance agent and insurance company's 24-hour hotline. Disposable cameras work well for documentation purposes.) Document the conditions that existed. Get contact info of all injured people and witnesses.

Employees who regularly drive their own vehicles on bank business should be trained to report accidents quickly. They, too, should be supplied with a disposable camera and insurance company contact info. They are covered by their own insurance for damage to their vehicle and their liability. The bank's liability is covered by the bank's insurance.

Follow Up with Adjusters

Stay in touch with your insurance company adjuster on the status of all claims. Your involvement may make the difference between a claim that drags on and one with a fast resolution.

Chapter 25

Workers' Compensation Claims Management Help

The workers' compensation claims process is largely determined by state law. Your insurance company will have forms and procedures to follow to report new incidents. Most have phone or Internet reporting systems.

Report Claims Quickly

Develop a claims reporting system in each of your locations. Employees should know whom to report incidents to. Managers should know where reports should be filed. Fast claim reporting to your insurer means an overall better outcome.

Have a Designated Physician/Medical Facility for Employee Injuries

Many states allow employers to designate a specific physician or medical center for the first few weeks of an employee's injury. This increased control allows specialists in workplace injuries to provide effective treatment for such injuries as soft tissue injuries (strained back) and repetitive motion claims (carpal tunnel and tendonitis issues).

Remote branches may need a separate designated medical facility.

Reporting claims promptly will improve your insurer's ability to manage claims. You end up saving premium dollars and your employee gets better care.

Follow Up with your Adjuster

If you average four or five workers' compensation claims a year, have one adjuster for all of your claims. Tell your insurer that you want to build a relationship with the adjuster handling your account. You want the adjuster to have a working knowledge of your approach to business and workers' compensation injuries. You want the adjuster to be a part of your team.

Review all open claims once a quarter with your agent and adjuster. The conversation is simple. Find out what has been done and what is going to be done. Follow up on any action plans. You want your claims to be handled as a priority by your insurance company.

Have a Return to Work Program

Work aggressively to bring employees back to work. Have a light-duty program available. Work with your employees' doctors and the adjuster to find meaningful work your injured employees can do.

Chapter 26

D&O and Employment Practices Claims Management Help

We all know when we have had an auto accident. A fire is a clear indication of a property claim. But when do you report a claim under your directors' and officers' or employment practices insurance policies?

<u>What is a Claim?</u>

Here are the definitions of a claim under one insurer's contract:

> *"Claim" means a director and officer claim, an entity claim, an employment practices claim, a lenders' liability claim, a securities claim, and a trust department claim.*
>
> *"Director and officer claim" means a demand or proceeding against a Director or Officer for a wrongful act other than an employment practices claim, a lenders' liability*

claim, a securities claim, or a trust-department claim.

"Employment practices claim" means a demand or proceeding against a Director or Officer or against the Company (if so indicated on the Declarations) for a wrongful act in connection with any actual or alleged:

Wrongful refusal to employ a qualified applicant for employment;

Wrongful failure to promote a qualified employee;

Wrongful demotion, negligent evaluation, negligent reassignment or wrongful discipline of any employee;

Wrongful termination of employment, including retaliatory or constructive discharge;

Harassment, coercion, discrimination or humiliation of an employee or applicant for employment as a consequence of race, color, creed, national origin, marital status, medical condition, gender, age, physical appearance, physical and/or mental impairment, pregnancy, sexual orientation or sexual preference; or

Oral or written publication of material that slanders, defames or libels an employee or violates or invades an employee's right of privacy.

"Entity claim" means a demand or proceeding against the Company (if so indicated on the Declarations) for a wrongful act other than an employment practices claim, a lenders' liability claim, a securities claim or a trust department claim.

The D&O policy deals with claims against the directors, officers, and the entity (the bank) for "wrongful acts."

Here is the same insurer's definition of wrongful act:

> *"Any actual or alleged act, error, neglect, omission, misstatement, misleading statement or breach of duty which shall have been committed or attempted, or which shall be alleged to have been committed or attempted ..."*

The policy goes on to say that claims must be reported to the insurer as soon as "practicable."

<u>When Should a Claim Be Reported?</u>

The easiest way to look at claim reporting is the following:

- Have you been sent or given a notice of a hearing, trial, or administrative proceeding for an act that may be covered by your insurance?

- Have you received a notice demanding compensation for a wrongful act?

If the answer is yes to either of the above, report the claim. That means that an attorney's letter stating that his client was fired unlawfully is a claim and must be reported to the insurer. A notice from your state's Equal Opportunity Board is a claim. Formal notice of a lawsuit is also a claim.

Review the definition of "claim" in your policy. Does the allegation have to be in writing?

Some insurers' definition of claim requires that the notice be in writing. The above policy does not. A customer alleging that a loan was improperly refused, who walks into your office and demands $10,000, is (under the definition above) a claim.

Failure to report a claim in a timely fashion can result in the insurance company denying coverage. In most cases, there is little reason to delay the reporting of a claim.

Notice that the above doesn't address the issue of claims under your deductible amount. Most banks have deductibles well over $50,000. Many of the allegations made against financial institutions are under the amount where insurance steps in. If there is even the slightest chance that the claim (payment to the claimant and defense costs) may exceed the deductible, report the claim.

Some insurers want all "claims" reported. Others only want to hear if you exceed the deductible. Work with your insurer to establish an understanding of what should be reported.

How Do You Report a Claim?

Most insurance policies will have a specific section dedicated to claim reporting. There will be a specific address, phone number, and fax number where you send a description of the allegations and the documents the claimant (or his attorney) presented to you.

Attorney Selection

Recalling my comments earlier in this book, each insurer has his own policy terms and conditions. The issue of selecting an attorney to assist in a claim is no different.

Under most bank directors' and officers' insurance, you will select your own attorney with your insurer's approval. Some policies will have a list of approved attorneys. You usually are still able to submit your own attorney for use.

Claim Settlement

Most policies do not allow the insured to settle claims without the approval of the insurance company. The result is a claim that the insurance company won't pay.

It seems to happen often in the banking world. A customer is "injured" by some action taken by the bank—loan turned down, improper allocation of funds to an account, an embarrassing check refusal—and the bank president decides to "do the right thing." While such action may be ethically correct, it also may jeopardize coverage under the bank's insurance.

Most insurer D&O claims staff are professionals. Due to the complexities of these claims, many of the adjusters are attorneys. Most of them welcome calls from an insured (and consultants, fortunately).

Take a moment and talk with your insurer before you offer a settlement—even on a small claim.

Chapter 27

Bond Claims Management Help

The Financial Institutions Bond responds to losses discovered during the policy period. The bank usually has 60 days from discovery of the event to report the loss to the insurance company.

Under most policies, if a claim is greater than 50 percent of the deductible amount, the claim must be reported to the insurer.

You have six months from discovery to file a proof of loss with your insurer.

I normally recommend bringing your insurer into bond claims quickly. While you may be experiencing a specific type of claim for the first time, your insurer has dealt with such issues hundreds of times. The claims department of your bonding company can save you many hours and a great deal of frustration. They can also help you "plug the leaks" so further losses are minimized.

Chapter 28

Loss Control Information

Controlling losses and minimizing the impact of losses usually equal money well spent. Here are some general hints:

Property Loss Control

- All locations should have walk-through inspections at least twice a year. Look for fire hazards such as the use of extension cords, broken or uncovered electrical outlets, paper materials near break room stoves, and accumulation of boxes or trash in storage areas. Are fire extinguishers up to date?

- Document the property you own. Have someone take pictures of the inside and outside of your offices and branch locations. Videos can work well too. Store the photos (or the digital images) away from your location. Make two copies. Store one in the main office and another in a branch location.

- Review fire extinguisher use with all employees at least once a year. Branch managers can use ten minutes in a staff meeting to go over proper use of the extinguishers at their location. No special training is needed for the trainer—read the instructions on the extinguisher.

- Regularly review evacuation procedures with all employees at all locations. Test alarms at least every three months.

- Inspect all locations at night looking for adequate lighting of parking areas and around the building. Proper lighting discourages vandalism.

- Consider installing video cameras in parking areas and locations susceptible to vandalism. Cameras help with slip and fall allegations, too.

- Are overhang and awning heights clearly marked? Consider installing warning barriers that will alert drivers before their too-tall vehicle hits the building.

- Are all the parking areas adjacent to your buildings equipped with parking guards to prevent vehicles from rolling into the side of the building?

- Are ATMs and other drive-up areas properly guarded against damage caused by vehicles coming too close?

Liability Loss Control

- Insist on clear walkways and sidewalks during winter storms.

- Use nonslip surfaces in entryways and corridors. Assign an employee at each location responsibility for keeping areas dry that are prone to tracked-in water during rainstorms.

- Remind branch personnel of the importance of responding quickly to slippery and hazardous conditions. (I've seen far too many reports of slip and fall accidents that begin with the phrase "Several people had slipped in the entryway over the morning

...." If only someone had put out a nonslip mat after the first person slipped!)

- Tiled restroom floors should be regularly treated to retain their nonslip characteristics.

- Instruct all branch managers on the proper procedure for handling slip and fall claims.

- Have a disposable camera available at all locations to document the conditions at the time of a reported injury.

- Be aware of food safety issues when snacks are put out for customers.

Workers' Compensation Loss Control

Preventing claims is the best approach to controlling your workers' compensation costs. "No claims" means low premiums.

- What services does your insurance company offer that can help you? Many insurers have training programs and training tapes you can use.

- Have an active safety committee with the authority to impact operations. No showcase committees—real, engaged, pragmatic work by a group of interested employees.

- Have regular walk-through inspections looking for hazards.

- Review the circumstances and facts of all incidents. Learn from past mistakes. What could have been done to prevent the problem?

- Lead by example. If your company's policy requires stretch breaks, then management needs to participate too—be out there with everyone else.

Employees watch the boss and follow his or her example.

- Make some aspect of safety a part of every employee meeting. It can be a review of fire extinguisher use or a discussion on the importance of having workstations ergonomically correct. There is a natural way to include safety in all aspects of the operation. Safety is a habit.

- Place emergency phone number stickers on the phones. Include emergency and non-emergency numbers for the police and fire departments. Don't forget about Poison Control as well. The national hotline of the American Association of Poison Control Centers is 1-800-222-1222. All these numbers are available in the front of most phone books.

- Consider ergonomic issues when designing work areas. What can be done to lessen strain and repetitive motion issues? How can lifting exposures be engineered to reduce claims?

Appendix 1

Insurance Terms

Accident An event or occurrence that is unforeseen and unintended.

Actual Cash Value Property insurance valuation method. The replacement cost of property damaged or destroyed at the time of loss, less depreciation.

ACV Actual Cash Value

ADA Americans with Disabilities Act

Additional Insured A person or organization that meets the definition of an insured within an insurance policy. The party is not named specifically but is insured due to a group or class. Employees, officers and directors, for example.

Additional Named Insured A person or organization, other than the first named insured, specifically named as an insured in the declarations of the policy.

Adjuster/Adjustor A person who investigates and settles losses for an insurance company. May be an employee of the insurer or an employee of an independent adjusting firm.

Advertising Injury Injury rising out of an offense

committed in the course of advertising activities. For example: libel, slander, defamation, violation of right of privacy, piracy, unfair competition, or infringement of copyright, title, or slogan.

Agent A legal representative of an insurance company. Role in the insurance transaction is to sell and service insurance. May be an employee. See also Independent Agent, Direct Writer Captive Agent.

Agent of Record See Broker of Record

Aggregate Limit A limitation in many liability policies stipulating the maximum amount available for the total of all claims paid in a period of time. Aggregates are usually annual.

Agreed Amount Endorsement An endorsement to property insurance policies that removes the penalty for coinsurance issues by agreeing that the amount of insurance meets any coinsurance requirements.

All Risk Antiquated term to describe the perils in a property insurance policy. It has been replaced by the term "Special Risk." Using "All" got insurers and agents into trouble. See Special Risk

Application A form completed by the insured and/or the agent, providing information used in the underwriting and pricing process. The application becomes a part of the insurance policy for many lines of insurance.

ARAP Rating system for assigned risk insurance programs managed by some states.

ARM Professional designation: Associate in Risk Management. A course of study including the management of risks using techniques other than insurance.

ARP Assigned Risk Plan

Assessable Policy An insurance policy that allows insurers to return to policyholders (as a group) for additional funds to cover losses of the group greater than anticipated.

Usually only utilized in mutual insurance companies and captive/self-insurance plans.

Assigned Risk Plan Also known as The Pool. This is a risk-sharing mechanism set up by states to provide insurance for employers where no standard insurance company is interested. The problem may be with the risk (poor loss experience) or with the state's workers' compensation system (the state insurance has set up a system where insurers feel that they cannot make money).

Audit Worksheet The document prepared by the auditor that outlines the payrolls of your company. In many cases, the worksheet will show the remuneration of each employee and the classification assigned to that individual. The information on the worksheet is used to calculate the final premium.

Audited Premium The final premium based upon the audited, actual payrolls.

Auditor See Premium Auditor.

Average Weekly Wage A wage figure used to determine the payout in lost wages to an employee injured in a workers' compensation loss.

B&M See Boiler and Machinery Policy.

Bailee An individual or entity that holds property of another. Examples are dry cleaners, jewelers, appliance repair firms, and computer repair firms.

Bailee Insurance Insurance on the property of others held by a bailee.

Bankers Blanket Bond See Financial Institutions Bond.

Bankers Professional Liability Insurance Coverage for wrongful acts by the bank in the relationship with a customer. Usually a section of the directors' and officers' insurance.

BI Bodily Injury

BII Business Income Insurance or Business Interruption Insurance

Binder An oral or written statement that insurance coverage has been placed in effect. Usually issued by an insurance agent or the insurance company pending the actual policy being issued.

Blanket Insurance A single limit of property insurance that insures multiple classes of property (buildings and contents) over multiple locations. Specific insurance provides specific coverage to a specific property. Blanket coverage lumps all property into one amount of insurance.

Bodily Injury Injury or death. Some liability policies include emotional distress in the definition.

Boiler & Machinery Policy Provides coverage for damage to equipment and machinery by mechanical breakdown, power surge, etc.

BOP Business Owners Policy

BOR See Broker of Record.

BPL Bankers Professional Liability

Broker An insurance professional who represents the insured in the insurance transaction. Sometimes used incorrectly as a synonym for agent.

Broker of Record Letter A form letter used to indicate to an insurance company a policyholder's preference as to which insurance agent will have exclusive rights to the insured. Excludes all other agents/brokers from accessing the insurance company in question for that policyholder.

Builder's Risk Insurance Property insurance designed to protect buildings under construction or renovation. The policy recognizes the unique issues and hazards of construction. The rating of the policy recognizes the increasing values at risk.

Burglary Breaking and entering into another person's building with felonious intent.

Business Income Insurance See Loss of Business Income.

Business Insurance A subset of insurance that applies to the risks and hazards of business ventures, as opposed to personal insurance.

Business Interruption Insurance Part of property insurance that pays for the lost profits and continuing expenses that result from physical damage to insured property caused by an insured peril.

See also Loss of Business Income, Extra Expense.

Business Owners Policy A package of insurance coverage providing both property and general liability insurance usually designed for smaller retail and office businesses.

Cafeteria Plan See Flexible Benefit Plan.

Cancellation Discontinuance of an insurance policy prior to policy expiration. May be at the request of the insured or by the insured's action (nonpayment of premium). In extreme cases, the insurance company cancels a policy for an increase in hazard. Cancellations are largely governed by state law.

Captive Agent An insurance agent who represents a single insurer or a single group of insurers. Captive agents may have to give their represented insurers first right of refusal or may be barred from accessing other insurers altogether.

Captive Insurance Company An insurance company owned by one or more non-insurance companies formed to provide insurance coverage for the owners.

Carrier The insurance company.

Casualty Insurance Classification of insurance dealing with losses caused by issues of liability through bodily injury, personal injury, wrongful acts, or property damage. Includes:

–Auto Insurance

–General Liability

–Workers' Compensation

–Professional Liability

–Directors' and Officers' Liability

–Fiduciary Liability

Many casualty insurers also write surety business.

Cede To transfer all or part of a risk written by an insurer to a reinsurer.

Certificate of Insurance Proof of the existence at a moment in time of an insurance policy. Usually prepared by an insurance agent, listing the coverage included in a program of insurance. Prepared for the information of a business associate of the insured—a subcontractor would have his agent issue a certificate to the general contractor.

Certified Insurance Counselor Professional designation in property and liability insurance administered by the Society of Certified Insurance Counselors.

CGL Commercial General Liability

CGL Policy See Commercial General Liability Policy.

Chartered Property and Casualty Underwriter Professional designation administered by the American Institute for Property and Liability Underwriters. The course of study includes extensive examinations covering the breadth of property and casualty insurance issues.

CIC See Certified Insurance Counselor.

Claims Made Refers to the trigger of liability coverage. An occurrence policy responds to events that happen (occur) during the policy period. Claims-made policies respond to lawsuits filed (the making of a claim) during the policy period.

Classification Work comp – see Employment Classification.

Closed Claim A claim that has been resolved. No further payments or treatments are expected.

CNP Closed No Payment. Used on loss runs and claim reports to indicate that no payment was made on a claim and the file has been closed.

COBRA Health insurance – stands for Consolidated Omnibus Budget Reconciliation Act.

Federal law that provides certain former employees, retirees, spouses, and dependent children the right to temporary continuation of health coverage at group rates.

Coverage is limited to 18 months.

Coinsurance A penalty clause in property insurance policies that requires a certain percentage of the property's value to be insured.

Example: A building with a replacement cost of $1,000,000 and an 80% coinsurance clause must be insured for at least $800,000 (80% of the $1,000,000 value), or a penalty is assessed at the time of a loss.

Coinsurance in health insurance means the percentage of a loss paid by the insurance company.

Liability insurance policies may have a coinsurance clause that denotes the percentage of the loss paid by the insurance company.

Collision Insurance Auto Insurance – coverage for damage caused to the insured vehicle by an automobile accident or upset of the vehicle. Damage caused by collision with an animal or bird is covered by comprehensive automobile insurance.

Combination Safe Depository Policy Covers losses to customers' property in a safe depository due to a loss or damage from actual, or attempted, burglary or robbery. Policies may exclude cash and coins.

Commercial Auto Policy Provides protection for liability arising out of the use of motor vehicles. Also provides physical damage coverage to specified vehicles (also known as comprehensive and collision coverage).

Commercial Crime Insurance Coverage forms used to insure against burglary, robbery, counterfeit currency for organizations other than banks and financial institutions.

Commercial Crime Policy Crime insurance used by general businesses. Banks use the Financial Institutions Bond.

Commercial General Liability Policy Provides coverage for bodily injury and property damage either from operations or products.

Commercial Lines Insurance A broad category of insurance indicating insurance for businesses, professionals, and commercial establishments.

Commercial Property Policy Coverage for buildings and contents.

Conditions Qualifications on the terms made by an insurance company – insured must pay premiums, insured must notify insurance company of claims, etc.

Coverage The scope of protection of an insurance policy. Used as a synonym for insurance.

CPCU See Chartered Property and Casualty Underwriter.

Credit Insurance Coverage against default by creditors. Insureds can protect all of their accounts receivable or specific creditors. Some credit insurance companies also provide credit watch and account receivable advisory services.

CSR See Customer Service Representative.

Customer Service Representative An employee of an insurance agency or company that provides administrative and customer support functions.

D&O Directors' and Officers' Insurance

Death Benefit Payment made to a policy beneficiary upon death.

Debit Card Coverage Can be included in the financial institutions bond. Provides coverage for loss resulting directly from the fraudulent use of a debit card to obtain cash or pay for products or services by gaining access to an electronic payment device, provided that such device, as part of the transaction, electronically verifies the customer's available funds in the customer's depository account at the insured's bank.

Debris Removal Clause Extends property insurance to include payment for the removal of the debris from an insured loss. Includes demolition, transportation, and disposal of the rubble.

Dec Declarations page – see Declarations.

Declarations The part of an insurance policy that specifically describes the limits, premiums, rates, names, and other information relative to a specific insured.

Deductible The part of a claim paid for by the insured. A $5,000 property deductible means that the insured pays the first $5,000 of any fire damage or other insured loss.

Difference In Conditions Policy A property insurance policy that provides additional perils such as earthquake and flood coverage.

Definitions The part of an insurance policy that defines many of the words used in the policy. Most policies highlight terms that are defined or place the term in quotation marks to indicate that the word is defined in the policy.

Depository Bond Bond (surety) to guarantee the safety of funds made by depositors and their availability for withdrawal as indicated in the terms of deposit. Generally used for municipalities and school districts.

DIC Difference in Conditions policy

Direct Writer An insurance company that does not work through independent insurance agents. Agents for direct writers are usually employees of the insurance company or in exclusive relationships with the insurance carrier. Liberty Mutual, State Farm, and Allstate are direct writers.

Directors' & Officers' Insurance Policy Provides coverage for allegations of third parties for mismanagement, failure to act properly, and other "wrongful acts" against directors and officers. Coverage also can be included for the bank, known as Entity Coverage

Discovery Period See Extended Reporting Period.

Dishonesty Insurance See Commercial Crime Policy.

Dividend A return of premium given after a policy has expired based on loss experience of the insured or of a group of insureds. Low losses result in higher dividends. Under most state laws insurers cannot guarantee dividends.

DOC See Drive Other Car coverage.

Domestic See Residence Employee.

Domestic Insurer An insurer domiciled in a state in which the insured's insurance is written.

Drive Other Car Coverage An endorsement to the commercial auto policy that extends coverage for individuals who are provided personal use of a company vehicle and are not covered by a personal auto policy.

Earned Premium Premium used in an insurance policy. In workers' compensation, premium is earned as the employer incurs payroll expense.

E-Banking Insurance Insurance designed to provide coverage for certain exposures unique to banking conducted over the Internet. Generally includes coverage for business interruption, copyright infringement, and public relations expense.

E-Commerce Insurance See E-Banking.

EDP Electronic Data Processing

EE Extra Expense

EL Employers' Liability

Employee Retirement Income Security Act U.S. federal law passed in 1974 that provides regulation over employee welfare plans – retirement funds, group insurance, pensions, etc.

Employers' Liability The second part of workers' compensation insurance policies. Provides protection from liabilities that arise out of the employment relationship but are not covered by workers' compensation. For example: a spouse of an employee who becomes ill because of chemical residues brought home on the employee's clothing.

Employment Classification The job code/description used to categorize employees and exposures.

Employment Practices Liability Insurance Liability insurance for acts of harassment, wrongful discharge, wrongful hiring, and discrimination. Also called EPLI.

Endorsement Additional policy coverage, conditions, or exclusions added to the insurance contract by the insurance company. Sometimes called a Rider.

Entity Coverage An extension of directors' and officers' insurance, providing coverage for legal actions against the insured entity.

EPLI Employment Practices Liability Insurance

ERISA See Employment Retirement Income Security Act.

ERISA Bond Provides the required protection for the assets of a retirement fund under the federal law known as ERISA

E-Risk Insurance See E-Banking.

Errors and Omissions Insurance See Professional Liability Insurance.

Estimated Premium Premiums determined at the beginning of a policy period based upon estimated payrolls. The insured pays for the policy based upon the estimated premium, and then the audit determines the final premium.

Excess and Surplus Lines See Surplus Lines.

Excess Liability Policy See Umbrella Liability.

Excess Loss Premium Factor A part of retrospective rating programs. A factor to compensate the insurer for limiting the effects of losses over a certain amount, $50,000 for example.

Excess Losses Part of the experience modification calculation. The amount of a loss that exceeds $5,000. See also Primary Losses.

Exclusion A part of an insurance contract that removes coverage for a specific set of circumstances. Flood is excluded from coverage on most property insurance policies.

Exclusive Agent See Captive Agent.

Experience Modification Factor A premium adjustment factor based upon the losses of a risk compared to losses of similar organizations. A ratio of expected losses to actual losses. Calculated by rating bureaus such as NCCI.

Experience Period Policy and claim periods used in the experience modification (mod); usually the oldest three of the past four years.

2006 mod is based on the data from years 2004, 2003, and 2002.

Exposure A vulnerability to loss.

Exposure Basis A unit of measuring exposure. In workers' compensation the exposure basis is remuneration. In the case of some rates for domestic help, the unit may be per employee.

A liability policy may use payroll, sales, or area as the basis of premium.

Extended Discovery Period See Extended Reporting Period.

Extended Reporting Period A provision included in claims-made liability insurance policies where, after the expiration or cancellation of a policy, the insured can extend the time to discover a claim that occurred prior to the end of the policy.

Also called a Tail or Discovery Period.

Extortion Extracting money or forcing actions based on a threat of harm. A part of most kidnap and ransom insurance policies.

Extra Expense Insurance A part of time element insurance that pays the increased costs necessary to get an insured back into business quickly after insured property is damaged by an insured peril.

Federal Employees Compensation Act Workers' compensation act for federal civilian government employees. Overseen by the U.S. government. Does not involve private insurers or state funds.

Federal Employers Liability Act (FELA) Applies to

railway workers who are exempt from workers' compensation statutes. Cases decided on the basis of employers' liability.

Fellow Servant Rule Archaic term used as a common-law defense for employers prior to workers' compensation laws. Held that employer was not liable for injuries to an employee if the injury was caused by a fellow employee.

Fidelity Bond See Commercial Crime Policy.

Fiduciary A person entrusted with property or the care of an asset.

Fiduciary Coverage See Fiduciary Liability Insurance.

Fiduciary Duty The duties expected of a fiduciary.

Fiduciary Liability Insurance Protects the fiduciaries, directors, and officers of employee welfare plans (group insurance, pension plans, 401k plans) against actual or alleged wrongful acts. Covers liabilities imposed by the federal law ERISA.

Financial Institutions Bond Pays for dishonest acts by employees or outsiders. Theft of money, forgery, counterfeit currency, damage by hackers, etc.

Fire Insurance Broad term used to describe building and personal property insurance protection.

Fire Legal Liability A part of the commercial general liability insurance policy that protects damage to the part of the building occupied by the insured that is damaged due to the insured's negligence. Usually called upon to protect tenants for damage to the portion of the building they rent.

First Named Insured The first person or organization listed on an insurance policy as an insured. First named insureds receive all policy notices and bills.

Flexible Benefit Plan An employee benefit plan that allows employees to select among the various group life, medical expense, disability, dental, and other plans that best meet their specific needs.

Flood Insurance Insurance against the peril of a general and temporary increase in the level of a stream, lake, river, or ocean.

Forced-Placed Insurance Property insurance designed to cover properties where the bank's customer (the mortgagee) has failed to buy his own property insurance. Usually written on a monthly reporting basis.

Foreign Insurer An insurer domiciled in a state other than the one in which the insured's insurance is written.

Form The contract of insurance that outlines terms and conditions of protection.

FRIP Fiduciary Responsibility Insurance Policy

Garagekeeper's Insurance Provides coverage for the liability of parking vehicles owned by others.

General Liability See Commercial General Liability.

GL General Liability

Governing Classification The employment class with the highest remuneration on a policy, except for standard exception classifications.

Group Self-Insurance Many employers banding together to insure their operations based on a pooling of exposures and risks. They become an insurer. Groups can be homogeneous (a bank workers compensation group) or heterogeneous (a plumber, a lumber yard, and a bank band together).

Guaranteed Cost A workers' compensation program that is not subject to adjustments in premiums based on losses. Guaranteed cost programs include audits, and premiums are adjusted based on changes to remuneration.

Hammer Clause A provision in a professional liability

policy or directors' and officers' insurance that limits the insurer's liability should the insured refuse to accept a settlement offer from the plaintiff.

Hard Market A description of the insurance marketplace used to indicate a period of increasing rates and constricting coverage/availability. A sellers' market. The opposite of a soft market.

Hazard A situation that presents a chance of loss or an increase in the severity of a potential loss.

Incurred Losses The total of amounts paid and amounts reserved.

Indemnification An agreement where one party agrees to provide protection for certain legal actions brought against the primary party by another.

Indemnity As to property insurance – legal principle that holds an insured should not collect more than what he or she lost in a claim.

As to work comp – lost time payments. As opposed to medical bills.

Indemnity Contract As to liability – a provision that the insurance company reimburses an insured after settlement of a claim.

Independent Adjuster A contractor of the insurance company who manages insurance claims for the insurance company.

Independent Agent An autonomous business that sells and services insurance policies as a representative of a variety of insurance companies.

Inland Marine Insurance A class of insurance covering articles in transit as well as the modes of transportation. Includes cargo, equipment, bridges, tunnels, art, jewelry, property owned by others, and other items.

Insurance A contractual agreement where an insurance company assumes the risks outlined in an insurance policy in return for payment of a premium.

Insurance Adjuster The person who manages the claim process for the insurance company. May be an employee of the insurer or a contractor hired by the insurer.

Insurance Carrier See Insurance Company.

Insurance Commissioner The top insurance regulatory official in a state. May be called a Superintendent.

Insurance Company A commercial enterprise formed to sell and service insurance policies.

Interstate Rating An experience modification that includes payroll and loss information from more than one state. Some states do not participate in interstate rating plans.

IRA-Keogh Errors & Omissions Policy Covers errors in the administration of IRA and Keogh plans.

K&R Kidnapping and Ransom Insurance

Kidnap, Ransom and Extortion Policy Pays moneys demanded either for kidnapping or the threat of kidnapping. Also pays for extortion with a threat to property.

Liability A legally enforceable obligation usually due to a breach of some duty or negligence.

Liability Insurance Insurance that responds to a breach or negligence of the insured to another party.

Liquor Liability Insurance Coverage designed to respond to liabilities arising out of the sale, manufacture or serving of alcoholic beverages.

Most commercial general liability policies exclude liquor liability claims only for those in the business of selling, manufacturing, or serving alcohol.

Longshoremen's and Harbor Workers' Act See United States Longshoremen's & Harbor Workers' Act.

Loss An accident or event that causes damage, injury, or illness.

Loss Adjustment Expenses Monies spent to investigate and settle losses.

Loss Control Practices and procedures used to minimize the severity of a loss. Also used to describe loss prevention activities.

Loss of Business Income A part of time element insurance that pays for the lost profits and continuing expenses after damage to insured property caused by an insured peril.

Loss Prevention Practices and procedures used to keep accidents from happening. Prevents frequency of loss. Also used to describe loss control activities.

Loss Ratio Incurred losses (and loss adjustment expenses) divided by net premiums earned. Measures profitability. A measure of losses compared to premiums.

Loss Reserves Estimated amounts for future payments of medical and wage payments for a specific claim.

Loss Run A record of losses for a policy period.

Lost Wages Amounts paid for wages lost by an employee due to a workers' compensation claim.

LTD Long-Term Disability

Manual Premium Calculated by multiplying payrolls by rate before application of any modification factors, schedule credits, or debits.

Manuscript Policy A unique policy customized to the needs and exposures of a specific insured and a specific insurance company.

Medical Payments General Liability – coverage for medical bills incurred by a third party at an insured location. Coverage is not dependent on the negligence of the insured.

Automobile – coverage for injuries to occupants of the insured vehicle caused by an auto accident.

Medical-Only Claims Workers' compensation claims where there is no lost time/wages.

Misrepresentation A false, incorrect, improper, or incomplete statement of a material fact, made in the application for an insurance policy. Constitutes fraud in many states.

Mod See Experience Modification.

Modified Premium The workers' compensation premium after the application of the experience modification, but before other credits/debits are applied.

Monopolistic A state workers' compensation system where no private insurers are allowed to compete for business.

MOP Manufacturers' Output Policy

Mortgage Impairment Policy Protects the bank's interest in properties mortgaged. Should a mortgage customer not purchase insurance (and the bank not know it), the policy will pay the bank's interest in the property should it be destroyed by a covered peril.

MP Medical Payments

Mutual Insurance Companies An insurance company owned by policyholders, as opposed to stockholders.

Named Insured Individual(s) and organization(s) listed on the declarations as insured.

National Association of Insurance Commissioners (NAIC) Association of state insurance regulators who administer state insurance rules and laws. NAIC promotes uniformity in regulation throughout the country.

NCCI The National Council on Compensation Insurance is the organization responsible in most states for administering classifications, experience modification factors, and collecting data used in ratemaking. NCCI is not connected with any state government. It is a rate and rulemaking organization funded by insurance companies that use their services. They report information to states and are certainly regulated by state insurance departments. It is not, however a government-run organization. They do act like it sometimes, though.

Net Premium Premiums after all fees, charges, and credits.

NOC As to work comp - see Not Otherwise Classified.

No-Fault Automobile Insurance An approach used by certain states to liability issues resulting from auto accidents. Injuries resulting from auto accidents are paid for by the insurance covering the vehicle occupied by the injured person, rather than who was negligent.

Noncancelable A policy feature that provides a guarantee of continuation of insurance at the insured's option. Insurers may adjust premiums, however.

Not Otherwise Classified As to work comp – a term used in the Scopes® classification manual and other rule books to indicate employment classifications that are not included in other class descriptions.

Occupational Disease An illness or disease resulting from a work hazard or condition.

Occupational Hazard A condition in a job or work environment that increases the peril of accident, sickness, or death.

Occurrence Defined by most liability policies as "an accident, including continuous or repeated exposure to substantially the same general harmful conditions."

Ocean Marine Insurance Insures boats, vessels, and cargo transported over water.

OD Occupational Disease

Ordinance or Law Insurance A part of property insurance that pays the increased cost of construction due to new zoning or building codes. Can also pay for demolition of the undamaged portion of a building that must be torn down due to violation of codes or ordinances. All coverage is triggered by a covered cause of loss plus the required action of laws or codes.

Other States Work comp – the section of the policy that describes how coverage will apply outside of the states listed in the classification page of your policy.

Package Policy Combining two or more insurance coverage sections into a single policy—property and liability coverages, for example. Homeowners and business owners' policies are package policies.

Partial Disability Work comp – impairment of a part of the body. May be permanent or temporary.

Payroll Audit Work comp – an examination of employer records to determine final remuneration in individual employment classifications for the purpose of determining policy premium. Performed by an auditor.

PD Property Damage

Peril A cause of loss – fire, lightning, hail, and robbery are examples of perils.

Permanent Partial Disability Partial impairment of a part of the body that is not reversible and will not heal—amputation of a finger, for example. May not impair work capacity for certain occupations. May remove an employee from the current occupation.

Permanent Total Disability Total loss of work capacity that is not reversible or will not heal.

Personal Injury Usually a part of the commercial general liability insurance policy. Provides coverage for libel, slander, false arrest, defamation of character. Actual definition varies by policy.

Personal Injury Liability Insurance Part of the commercial general liability insurance policy that provides protection for libel, slander, defamation, or violation of right of privacy; and wrongful entry, eviction, or other invasion of right of private occupancy.

Personal Injury Protection (PIP) Auto insurance – see No-Fault.

Personal Lines Insurance coverage in property and casualty insurance for families and households—personal auto coverage and homeowners insurance, for example.

PI Personal Injury

Policy The insurance contract. It spells out the terms, conditions, and exclusions of the insurance provided by the insurance company.

Policy Term The period of time that the insurance policy is in force.

Policyholder The person or organization that owns the insurance policy.

Pollution A cause of loss that is excluded by most property and liability insurance policies. Usually requires a special pollution liability insurance policy.

Pool See Assigned Risk Plan.

Premium The price of insurance for a specified risk for a specified period of time.

Premium Auditor Work comp – an individual who performs the audit of remuneration at the end of a policy period. May be an employee of the insurance company or a contractor hired by the insurance company.

Premium Discount Work comp – a premium credit based on the size of the premium paid.

Premium Finance Finance arrangement for the insured to make payment of the insurance premium.

Primary Insurance The insurance policy that is responsible for paying the first part of a loss. Excess policies pay after primary policies pay.

Primary Losses Work comp – part of the experience modification calculation. The first $5,000 of any loss. See also Excess Losses.

Product Liability Insurance Protection from legal actions against an insured for bodily injury and property damage caused by a product sold, manufactured, processed, or provided by the insured.

Professional Liability Insurance Insurance against negligent damage caused by a wrongful act of the insured. Usually excludes bodily injury and property damage.

Also called malpractice insurance.

Also called errors and omissions insurance.

Proof of Loss Presentation by the insured of documentation of the extent of a claim. Usually used in property insurance policies as a condition. Insurers must respond (pay) within a certain time to the presentation by the insured of a proof of loss.

Property Damage Physical damage to tangible property.

Property Insurance Insurance protection for loss of tangible property owned by or in the care of the insured. Includes buildings, personal property, stock, inventory, and time element insurance.

Property Policy See Commercial Property Policy.

Protection and Indemnity Insurance Specialized insurance for boats and commercial vessels. Responds to the unique exposures of maritime law and federal laws such as the Jones Act.

Public Adjuster A person or firm that is a representative of the insured in a claim for insurance benefits.

Rating Bureau Work comp – an organization that compiles statistical and rate-making information to determine premiums. See NCCI. Non-NCCI states have their own rating bureaus. See the appendix of this document for a listing of NCCI states and the regulatory agencies for workers' compensation in each state.

RC Replacement Cost

Registered Mail Insurance Provides insurance for loss, damage, or destruction of securities and other important or valuable papers during shipment.

Rehabilitation Benefits Benefits payable to return an injured worker to work after a work-related injury or illness.

Reinsurance Insurance purchased by insurance companies to provide a risk transfer mechanism. Also used by self-insurers and self-insured groups.

Remuneration Payroll and other compensation paid to employees. Used to calculate premiums.

Renewal The reestablishment of an insurance policy after the expiration of a prior term of coverage.

Replacement Cost Property valuation method that uses the cost of replacement of an item or the cost of new construction without any deduction for depreciation.

Reservation of Rights A response to a claim whereby the

insurance company defends a case without any commitment as to the coverage provided by a policy.

Reserve Amount expected to be paid on a claim that is not resolved or closed.

Residence Employee Work comp – a person who performs full- or part-time household services.

Residual Market See Assigned Risk Plan.

Retention Amount of a claim paid by the insured. The term is usually used in liability insurance. Similar to a deductible

Retention Plan A loss sensitive insurance plan that adjusts the premium up or down based on losses and associated costs.

Retrospective Rating A loss sensitive workers' compensation insurance program where adjustments are made to premiums after policy expiration. Adjustments can go up or down subject to premium minimums and maximums.

Rider See Endorsement.

Risk 1) Exposure to loss 2) An insured 3) A portion of an insured operation

Risk Management The process of addressing in a systematic way the hazards and exposures of an organization. Risks can be avoided, reduced, transferred, and retained.

Insurance transfers the risk (or a part of it) to an insurance company.

Risk Retention Group Alternative risk financing tool where similar businesses band together to share risks. Usually utilizes reinsurance and individual retentions along with regimented loss control and claims management process. Meets the requirements of the Risk Retention Act of 1986.

Safe Depository See Combination Safe Depository.

Schedule Credit/Debit Premium adjustment factors applied at the discretion of insurance company underwriters and based upon individual characteristics of the risk. Issues such as managed care, quality of management, loss control efforts, and the insurance company's appetite for the risk are included.

Scopes® Manual Work comp – a publication of NCCI that outlines the definitions of the 600 plus employment classifications.

Second Injury Fund Work comp – a mechanism set up by states to minimize the impact of re-injuries. The theory is that employers will be reluctant to hire previously injured workers without such a system.

Sometimes funded by surcharges on insurers for death claims where there are low medical bills.

Self-Insurance Retention of the risk usually in a formal, calculated way. In workers' compensation, state regulations impose financial and administrative qualifications. May involve reinsurance or very large deductibles to cover catastrophic losses.

Self-insurance isn't really insurance—you are retaining the risk.

Self-Insured Retention See Retention.

Short-Rate Penalty A penalty assessed when an insurance policy is cancelled by the insured in the middle of a policy period. Workers' compensation short-rate penalties are high in the early months and gradually decline through the policy period. Short-rate penalties in other property and casualty policies are usually 10% of the unearned premium.

Side A Coverage within a directors' and officers' insurance policy that pays for claims against individual directors or officers when corporate reimbursement isn't allowed.

Side B Coverage within a directors' and officers' insurance policy that pays for claims against individual directors or officers when corporate reimbursement is allowed.

Side C Coverage within a directors' and officers' insurance policy that pays for claims against the bank. Also referred to as entity coverage.

Sliding Scale Dividend A dividend plan that varies the size of the dividend payment based on the loss ratio of the insured.

Soft Market A description of the insurance marketplace used to indicate a period of declining rates and expanding coverage/availability. A buyers' market. The opposite of a hard market.

Sole Remedy Workers' compensation is said to be the sole remedy for an employee's workplace injuries. In most states, employees may not seek payment from employers outside of workers' compensation for an employer's negligence or liability for an injury.

Special Risk A type of property insurance policy where all perils (causes of loss) are insured except those that are excluded by the policy. Some common exclusions: flood, earthquake, animals, nuclear, and deterioration.

STAMP Bond Securities Transfer Agents Medallion Program – provides signature guarantee.

Standard Exception Classifications Work comp – employment classifications that are allowed on most policies in addition to the primary business classes.

Clerical, Sales, and Driver are common standard exceptions.

Standard Markets Insurance companies that are not surplus lines insurers.

Standard Policy An insurance policy used by a preponderance of insurance companies to cover similar exposures and operations.

Standard Premium Work comp – premium after application of the experience modifier and schedule credits or debits, but before premium discount.

State Fund A workers' compensation insurance system run by a state governmental agency. May be competitive with private insurers or monopolistic. Also synonymous with assigned risk fund or pool.

STD Short-Term Disability

Strict Liability Liability that comes out of an exposure that is so onerous that negligence need not be proven. Blasting within a city, the keeping of wild animals.

Subrogation The procedure under which an insurance company recoups losses paid from the insurer of the negligent or responsible party. For example, a workers' compensation insurer may subrogate against the auto insurer of the driver who caused an accident in which an employee is injured.

Surety Bond An agreement that guarantees that the principal will fulfill its obligations to the obligee.

Surety – bonding company.

Principal – party performing the work.

Obligee – entity for whom the principal is working to whom the surety is obligated.

Surplus Lines Insurance written by non-admitted insurance companies.

Tail Coverage See Extended Reporting Period.

Temporary Partial Disability A condition where an injured worker's capacity is impaired for a time, but he is able to continue working at reduced capacity. Full recovery is expected.

Temporary Total Disability A condition where an injured worker is unable to work at all while he is recovering from injury. Full recovery is expected.

Terrorism Risk Insurance Act Federal law outlining the taxpayer-funded reinsurance provided for certain types of terrorism losses.

Time Element Insurance A subset of property insurance that pays the lost profits, continuing expenses, and increased expenses caused by an insured peril. Usually triggered by damage to insured property.

See Loss of Business Income.

See Extra Expense Insurance.

Tort A civil wrong other than a breach of contract.

TRIA Terrorism Risk Insurance Act

Trust Department Errors & Omissions Policy Provides protection for claims made against a bank for losses resulting from an error or omission by the trust department while performing trust functions.

Twisting Inaccurate or incomplete insurance policy descriptions used to entice the surrender or cancellation of an insurance policy in favor of another policy.

U&O Use and Occupancy (antiquated term)

UIM Under-Insured Motorist

UM Uninsured Motorist

Umbrella Liability A form of excess insurance that provides additional limits of liability protection as well as increasing the breadth of the coverage provided.

Umbrella Liability Policy Provides extra liability coverage above the general liability, auto liability, and employers' liability coverage. Also known as excess liability.

Underlying Policies The basic liability insurance policies accessed before excess or umbrella liability policies. Usually include auto liability, general liability and employer's liability.

Underwriter 1) An insurance company

2) The individual who performs underwriting for an insurance company

Underwriting The process an insurance company goes through to classify, analyze, and price an insurance policy.

Unearned Premium The difference between the premium paid and the earned premium.

Uninsured/Underinsured Motorist Coverage Auto – pays the policyholder for injuries to occupants of the insured vehicle if the accident was caused by a driver who has too little or no liability insurance.

Unit Stat Card Work comp – a form filed with a rating bureau by an insurance company to report remuneration and losses on a specific policy. Used to calculate the experience modification. Usually submitted based on losses shown at the 6-month point in a policy.

United States Longshoremen's & Harbor Workers' Compensation Act Federal workers' compensation law that stipulates compensation for those who work in harbors and on wharves.

U.S.L. & H. See United States Longshoremen's and Harbor Workers' Compensation Act.

Voluntary Compensation An endorsement to the standard workers' compensation insurance policy; extends coverage to employees not required to be covered under the state's workers' compensation law. Farm workers, domestic help, business owners, for example. Usually has nothing to do with volunteers. The term refers to the voluntary addition of normally uncovered individuals.

Voluntary Market The standard insurance market where insurers offer coverage on a competitive basis with no pressure from government. Assigned risk insurance programs (auto or workers' compensation) are involuntary markets.

Insurance written outside of any assigned risk plan.

WC Workers' Compensation

Workers' Compensation 1. A state-mandated program of benefits for injured workers

2. An insurance policy designed to provide benefits based on a state's workers' compensation law

Workers' Compensation Insurance Pays benefits as provided by state law for work-related injuries or diseases. The policy also provides protection for other types of work-related incidents.

Appendix 2

Peer Data

Professional Liability – Peer Data – December 2006

	Total Bank Asset Size				
	<$50M	$51M-$150M	$151M-$300M	$301M-$500M	$501M-$1,000M
Directors and Officers Liability	$1.7M	$2.5M	$3.7 M	$5.0M	$6.7M
Broad Form Company Liability	$1.1M	$1.7M	$2.4 M	$3.2M	$4.2M
Employment Practices Liability	$900K	$1.2M	$1.7M	$2.0M	$2.7M
Internet Banking Liability	$850K	$1.0M	$1.2 M	$1.4M	$1.7M

Data provided by Progressive Casualty Insurance Company. Based on 1,700 community banks in all 50 states. Used with permission. See www.banks.progressive.com for full and updated peer data information.

Financial Institutions Bond – Peer Data – December 2006

	Total Bank Asset Size				
	<$50M	$51M-$150M	$151M-$300M	$301M-$500M	$501M-$1,000M
Fidelity	$1.4M	$2.1M	$3.1M	$4.1M	$5.8M
Forgery	$910K	$1.3M	$2.2M	$3.1M	$4.4M
Securities Forgery	$890 K	$1.3M	$2.1M	$3.0M	$4.3M
Computer Systems	$1.1M	$1.5M	$2.6M	$3.4M	$5.1M
Fraudulen t Mortgage	$680 K	$1.0M	$1.6M	$1.9M	$2.9M
Stop Payment	$60K	$80K	$100K	$110K	$140K
Transit Cash	$420K	$640K	$970K	$1.2M	$1.7M
ATM	$50K	$55K	$70K	$75K	$150K
Safe Depository	$560K	$810K	$1.2M	$1.5M	$1.8M

Data provided by Progressive Casualty Insurance Company. Based on 1,700 community banks in all 50 states. Used with permission. See www.banks.progressive.com for full and updated peer data information.

Appendix 3

Agent Qualification Questionnaire Form

See Chapters 20 and 21 for instructions on using this form.

<Insert Your Bank's Name Here>

Note: This document is to be used to gather information on agents and brokers you are considering for a bid or broker selection process. Email me at Scott@ScottSimmonds.com for a free copy of this document in Microsoft Word format.

Introduction

We are investigating a possible change in our bank's insurance relationships. As part of that analysis we are reviewing the qualifications of a select number of brokers. Please answer all questions completely. Attachments may be used as necessary.

Using the information you provide and the information we obtain from other agents/brokers, we will decide whether to bid, select an exclusive broker, or continue our existing relationship.

If you have questions or need additional information please contact:

<Contact Name>

<Contact Phone>

<Contact Fax>

<Contact Email>

Please return your reply to this questionnaire by email, fax, mail, or courier to:

<Name & Address>

Your reply to this questionnaire is due by noon on <Date>.

About Us

Include a narrative of your bank here. At a minimum, provide at least the following:

Subsidiary and holding company names

Date established

List of locations

Web site address

Overview of the business, including subsidiaries

Estimated annual payroll

Number of employees

Current insurance broker's name

Current insurance company

Approximate total annual premiums paid

Basic Agency/Brokerage Info

Please provide information on your agency. Feel free to use additional sheets or marketing material to help us get to know you.

Name of agency/brokerage:

Address of agency/brokerage office for this account:

Main phone:

Fax:

Web site address:

Normal business hours: Time zone:

Date firm established:

Please provide a brief history of your organization.

Total number of employees:

Approximate firm revenues:

Please provide information on the individuals who will be responsible for this account. Attach résumés of each person.

Name	Title

List other clients handled by the above team.

What are your firm's strengths compared to similar and competing insurance organizations?

List the top five insurance companies (by premium) in your agency.

Is your agency licensed in all states where we have operations?

Is the account executive licensed in all states where we have operations?

Does your agency carry professional liability insurance in excess of $1,000,000?

Provide at least three references who are current clients and who are in the financial services industry. Provide account name, contact person, and telephone number. We will be contacting all three. Please let your references know that we will be calling.

Name	Company	Phone	Email

Services You Will Provide

Describe your account review process.

Will you provide a regularly updated summary of current insurance, including coverage limits, premiums, and policy terms?

Describe the loss control services you will provide.

Describe the claims management services you will provide.

How will you be compensated for the services and insurance policies you provide?

Is it your custom to disclose commissions, fees, bonuses, and other remuneration from insurance companies and other service organizations?

What insurance companies would you consider using for our account? Please note this is for information only. We are not assigning insurance companies at this time.

Feel free to reference other material and to provide additional marketing material along with this document.

Appendix 4

Bid Summary Matrix

The following forms are samples intended to provide an idea of the information needed to review and compare bid proposals. They are not intended to outline all coverage features and exclusions.

Email me at Scott@ScottSimmonds.com for a free copy of this document in Microsoft Word format.

Property

	Insurer A	**Insurer B**	**Insurer C**
Blanket Building & Personal Property Limit			
Agreed Amount?			
Coinsurance			
Special Perils?			
Property Valuation			
Flood Coverage			
Flood Limitations			
Flood Deductible			
Earthquake Coverage			
Earthquake Deductible			
Property Deductible			
Windstorm Deductible			
Debris Removal			
Building Ordinance			
Improvements and Betterments			

Personal Property of Others			
Personal Property Off-Premises			
Off-Premises Services			
Boiler & Machinery			
Accounts Receivable			
Computer Equipment			

Business Interruption

	Insurer A	Insurer B	Insurer C
Business Income			
Extra Expense			
Coinsurance			
Blanket All Locations?			
Agreed Amount			
Maximum Period of Indemnity			
Peril of Service Interruption			
Loss of Rental Income			

Casualty

	Insurer A	**Insurer B**	**Insurer C**
Occurrence CGL Form			
Occurrence Limit			
Aggregate Limit			
Fire Legal Limit			
Per Location Aggregate			
Premium Basis			
Auto Limit of Liability			
Non-Owned Auto Coverage?			
Drive Other Car Coverage			
Employees as Insured on Auto Policy			
Common Insurer for GL/Auto			
Owned Watercraft or Aircraft			
Pollution/Environmental Liability			
Workers' Compensation States			
Employers' Liability			

Limits			
Umbrella			

Financial Institutions Bond

	Insurer A	Insurer B	Insurer C
Fidelity			
On Premises			
In Transit			
Forgery and Alteration			
Securities Forgery			
Check Kiting			
Claims Expense			
Audit Expense Rider			
Computer Systems Coverage – Fraud			
Counterfeit Check			
Counterfeit Currency			
Destruction by Hacker			
Destruction by Virus			
Extortion			
Fraudulent Mortgage			
Injury/Death Indemnity			
Lost Instrument Bond			

Trading Loss			
Transit Cash Letter			
Unattended ATM			
Unauthorized Signature			
Fax Wire Fraud			
Telephone Wire Fraud			

Directors' and Officers'

	Insurer A	**Insurer B**	**Insurer C**
Policy Limit			
Entity Coverage Included in Policy Limit			
Brokerage/Advisory Services			
Employment Practices Liability			
Trust E&O			
Insurance Agent E&O			
Coverage Trigger			
Lender Liability Limit			
IRA/Keogh			
Fiduciary			
Discovery Premium			
Employment Practices			
EPL Definitions			
Are Above Limits Separate Limits or Do They Deplete The Aggregate?			

Premiums

	Insurer A	**Insurer B**	**Insurer C**
Property			
Inland Marine			
Machinery Breakdown			
Liability			
Crime			
Auto			
Workers' Comp			
Umbrella			
Financial Institution Bond			
Safe Depository			
Directors and Officers			
Employment Practices			
Fiduciary			
Internet Liability			
Mortgage Impairment			
STAMP Bond			

Forced Placed Property			
Lenders Single Interest			
Service Fees?			

Agency Service Expectations

	Insurer A	Insurer B	Insurer C
Frequency of Account Review			
Claims Department			
Producer Involvement in Account?			
Extent of Loss Control Services			
Phone/Email Return Policy?			

Insurer Issues

Complete for each insurer offered by a participating agent.

Insurer name: ________________________________

Offered by agent: ______________________________

Best Rating: __________ Weiss Rating: __________

Underwriting office location: ______________________

Claims office location: __________________________

Loss control location: ___________________________

Will one adjuster handle all claims; a single contact person?

What loss control services will be offered?

Are audits handled by the insurer or by an audit company?

About Scott Simmonds

Scott Simmonds, CPCU, ARM, CMC is a 27-year veteran of the insurance business. He has provided insurance advice and counsel to well over one thousand companies, large and small, throughout the US.

After graduating from Babson College, Wellesley, Massachusetts, Simmonds entered the insurance business. In 1987 he received the Certified Insurance Counselor designation from the Society of CIC. In 1995, Simmonds completed his studies to qualify for the Chartered Property and Casualty Underwriter designation conferred by the American Institute for CPCU. He completed the requirements for the Insurance Institute of America's Associate in Risk Management designation in 2005.

Simmonds' insurance work has involved companies in a wide range of industries. He has handled insurance and risk management issues for public and private corporations, including many with international operations. His work includes nonprofits, banks, manufacturing organizations, hospitality companies, municipalities, and schools. He is licensed in property, casualty, life, and health insurance consulting.

Scott's writing and comments have appeared in the Wall Street Journal, Forbes, Portland Press Herald, Mainebiz,

Fortune, Money, Inc. Magazine, the New York Times, Investors Business Daily, Kiplinger's, the Los Angeles Times, and countless trade publications.

The Institute of Management Consultants awarded Scott the Certified Management Consultant designation. CMC represents evidence of the highest international standards of consulting competence and adherence to the ethical canons of the profession.

Scott is a member of the Society for Advancement of Consulting, an organization accepting only the top 1% of consultants nationwide. He is the first insurance consultant granted membership in this prestigious organization. The society recognized his accomplishments in insurance by awarding "Board Approved" status. Scott was only the nineteenth consultant worldwide afforded this honor.

Simmonds lives in Saco, Maine, with his family. He is a past president of the trade association, Maine Association of Professional Consultants, and past president of the Biddeford-Saco Rotary Club. He is also active in many trade associations and serves on the adjunct faculty at the York County Community College teaching small business management.

Scott Simmonds, CPCU, ARM, CMC
Insurance from an Unbiased Point of View
(207) 284-0085 Fax (801) 991-4027
Scott@ScottSimmonds.com
www.ScottSimmonds.com
www.BankInsuranceHelp.com

Index

A

B

C

D

E

F

G

H

I

K

L

M

N

O

P

R

S

T

U

V

W